Born Down
by the Water

The Collected Stories
of Robert C. Parsons

National Library of Canada Cataloguing in Publication

Parsons, Robert Charles, 1944-
Born down by the water : the collected stories of Robert C. Parsons.

Includes index.
ISBN 1-894463-52-8

I. Newfoundland and Labrador--History--Anecdotes. I. Title.

FC2161.8.P37 2004   971.8   C2004-902996-7

Cover photo © Dale wilson

PRINTED IN CANADA

FLANKER PRESS LTD.
P.O. BOX 2522, STATION C
ST. JOHN'S, NL CANADA A1C 6K1
TOLL FREE: 1-866-739-4420 TELEPHONE: (709) 739-4477 FAX: (709) 739-4420
INFO@FLANKERPRESS.COM
WWW.FLANKERPRESS.COM

Canadä
We acknowledge the financial support of the Government of Canada through the Book Publishing Industry Development Program (BPIDP) for our publishing program.

Born Down
by the Water

The Collected Stories
of Robert C. Parsons

Flanker Press Ltd.
St. John's, NL
2004

Dedication

To all editors, whose work, at one time or another, has
intersected with my own – great people, every one

TABLE OF CONTENTS

AUTHOR'S NOTE

Most selections in *Born Down by the Water* are articles and stories which were published over the years in various magazines and newspapers; mainly *The Newfoundland Quarterly, Legion Magazine, Newfoundland Lifestyle, Downhomer, The Evening Telegram,* and *The Southern Gazette.* I feel that many readers would not have read these stories before and that many would like to.

To compile *Born Down by the Water* I searched the various magazines for the selections, cleared copyright where necessary or possible, and revised some pieces. Six stories appear for the first time in this book. Since my community history, *Vignettes of a Small Town* (1997), is primarily of local interest and limited readership, I included one story from there which I felt would have a wider appeal.

Readers will also note that in the past most of my material is marine-related, specifically of ships and wrecks. *Born Down by the Water* has several shipwreck tales, but it also has other non-fiction stories of other natural and human calamities: tidal wave, fire, riot, murder and war.

For most selections, there are brief explanatory notes saying why or how the idea for a story originated, when and where the article was published, and other peculiarities regarding the writing and publication process. These appear as author's notes at the end of the book.

Born Down by the Water is dedicated to the editors and publishers who, over the years, have taken my offerings, shaped them up and presented them for others to read. I also know that my work is directly related to the philosophy contained in Matthew 21:22 KJV.

The title, *Born Down by the Water*, reflects the nature of most items in this collection. I was born and grew up – like most Newfoundland and Labrador people – within a few feet of the Atlantic Ocean. The stories were influenced, like me, by that great element of nature forever stamping at our doorstep.

Sea Stories

Bound Home for Newfoundland

Ask anyone who lived through the Great Depression years, the nineteen thirties, and they'll tell you how tough it was to survive. Most Newfoundland and Labrador people refer to the times as "The Dirty Thirties" when employment and money were scarce, not only in Newfoundland, but everywhere in North America.

By 1938 Philip Osmond, after nine years of odd jobs and trying to find work in Toronto, had enough. He decided to go back to Newfoundland. Even if there was no ready job waiting, at least back home living was easier; one could grow vegetables, do some logging, fish, build on available land and family and friends were always willing to help. Philip's wife had recently passed away and he had several children to support. He hit upon a bold plan: he'd build his own boat as cheaply as possible and sail back, taking his family with him.

Philip, born in Greenspond, was a jack-of-all-trades. He could make or fix just about anything, but in his younger years had done a little carpentry and fished. Between January and May1938, Philip built his sturdy boat, or "Newfoundland-style yacht" as he called it, in his yard in Toronto. He named his craft *F. Lydia* in honour of his late wife, Florence Lydia (Sturge of Wesleyville) Osmond.

He had a little experience in shipbuilding, limited to what he had observed and helped with as a youth in Newfoundland, but with innate skill and determination he constructed his 31-foot long boat from salvaged plank and other bits of wood. Toronto municipal authorities also allowed him to trim and cut unwanted elm trees out of a park in Don Valley, Toronto. From this he fashioned the stem post, knees, stanchions, planks. The 21-foot keel was Don Valley oak, cut, hewed and planed by hand. A junk-yard provided five dollar second or third-hand car engine, duly installed before the yacht was decked over. Below deck *F. Lydia* had two cabins, one aft and one forward.

The Osmond family lived on Augusta Avenue in Don Valley, about one and a half miles from Lake Ontario. As the project began to take shape quite a few residents and neighbors stopped to view the compact craft. It is said that a gentleman, a stranger, walked past Philip's home and small shipyard occasionally and would enquire on the progress of his project.

One day the man asked, "Once built, how are you going to get your ship down to the lake?" Osmond could only reply that when the time came, he and the Lord would find a way.

Sterling Osmond built two models of *F. Lydia* which are now in the home of his wife Mrs. Mildred Osmond, Lethbridge. Sterling passed away in 2003.

And he did. After the little yacht was finished and read-ied for launching, the same gentleman sent a large lift crane and truck or trailer and *F. Lydia* was taken to Lake Ontario near the Toronto waterfront. In the early morning sunrise – to avoid traffic – the procession angled down Bathurst, College Street to the launch site onto an airplane slip opposite John Street.

There were six Osmond children: Rita and Jerry, who were older, stayed behind in Toronto. Johnny, the designated ship engineer who was about 21 years old, agreed to sail as far as Quebec and then to return to Toronto where he was betrothed to his girl. Daughter Ivy, 23, sons Sterling, 13, and eleven-year-old Bert sailed with their father to Newfoundland.

In the small hold and cramped cabin space (*F. Lydia* was four and half feet deep) the Osmond family stored all their material possessions and supplies necessary to get them to Newfoundland. In the small stove in the after cabin, Ivy cooked, albeit she had to stoop considerably or kneel.

A Toronto yacht club provided sails, much too large, but they were cut to size, hemmed or footed with rope in the living room of the Augusta Avenue home. To save on unnecessary expense, resourceful Philip didn't plan to use the engine much except when there was an emergency or if there was no wind.

It was a long and hazardous voyage of approximately 2000 kilometres (1250 miles) just to reach the Strait of Belle Isle, but on May 27, 1938, the family waved goodbye to the few family and friends gathered on the Toronto dock.

On June 2, the family made one of the first major stops. At Bowmanville, Ontario, two cedar masts – the mainmast measured 28 feet – were cut, stepped and the sails bent on.

By early June the Osmonds were well down Lake Ontario and sailing east along the St. Lawrence River. At Quebec City, the engine's faulty intake system was repaired and Johnny wished "Bon Voyage" to his siblings and father. Watching *F. Lydia* sail away, he must have had second thoughts for no doubt his help and mechanical mind would be missed. Would they ever complete the arduous trip without him? And would he ever see his father, brothers and sister again?

Johnny's departure meant Sterling was now his father's main helper, or "second hand" as he called himself. In his personal memoirs of the voyage, Sterling recalled passing through the locks of the St. Lawrence Seaway and remembered that his father, an excellent navigator who studied the local charts, avoided the treacherous shoals of the St. Lawrence River.

When *F. Lydia* reached the wide expanses of sea at the mouth of the St. Lawrence, Philip realized he could not take any foolhardy chances of travelling up the Quebec shore, along the treacherous Gulf of St. Lawrence and across the Strait of Belle Isle without a lifeboat or "go-ashore" boat. On July 15, he put into Natashkwan, near Anticosti Island, for a few days and, with planks obtained at a sawmill in Eskimo Harbour, built a flat-bottomed boat which was towed behind *F. Lydia* to Newfoundland. At this point the propellor was removed for the yacht laboured, dragging an unused propellor and towing a boat.

Newspaper *Toronto Star* took this photo of Philip. The reporter (believed to be Gordon Sinclair who later was a panelist on CBC's long-running show "Front Page Challenge") was dockside when *F. Lydia* left Toronto on May 27, 1938, for Newfoundland. Sterling recalled that a reporter came to the launching, but was knocked "arse over kettle" into the water. Gruff Philip told him, "If you can't do any better than that, stay out of the way."

Philip had already decided to sail northeast along the Quebec shore to Sept-Isles, Harrington Harbour, then Blanc Sablon and cross over to the Great Northern Peninsula. Going was slow as *F. Lydia* hopped from dawn to dusk from one harbour to another. At Cape Bauld and in the Straits he realized he would encounter other Newfoundland schooners and seamen, perhaps some whom he knew.

In Forteau on August 21 the Osmond crew cleared customs for they were about to cross the strait and enter Newfoundland, not a part of Canada at that time. In essence *F. Lydia* was entering a "foreign" country at last, touching land first at Cook's Harbour on the tip of the Great Northern Peninsula. It was August 27.

Meanwhile, on June 16 the amazing story and a photo of *F. Lydia* with its four passengers were featured in a PEI newspaper, *The P.E. Island Agriculturist*. There it said Osmond expected to complete the journey in 15 days. On that estimate the papers were well off – over 90 days had already passed.

Having reached Newfoundland's Cape Bauld, Philip still would have had a further voyage of another five or six hundred kilometers along the coastline to his final destination, northeastern Newfoundland. Other than enduring a vicious gale and a near shipwreck at the Horse Islands off White Bay (where Mrs. Elizabeth Bath and her family cared for the children for four days while Philip mended sail), the determined skipper encountered no difficulties on the journey. As a Newfoundlander, he was totally at home on the water and had the inbred skills and confidence to accomplish what he set out to do.

Word soon got around in northeastern Newfoundland; folks knew the yacht was coming. Philip approached Valleyfield-Wesleyville, Bonavista Bay, on September 5.

Outside the town a flotilla of amazed and delighted family, friends and fishermen met *F. Lydia* and gave the becalmed yacht a tow. At Valleyfield and Wesleyville were his late wife's people, the Sturges and Philip's maternal family, the Strattons. There are friends and relatives today who well recall going down to the Valleyfield government wharf to view "the trim little yacht, all schooner-rigged," as they called it.

Philip finished his 108-day odyssey in Salmon Cove, Conception Bay, where he settled down for awhile with his people. Sterling, in his memoirs, recalled:

> Dad couldn't remember much about the landmarks for Salmon Cove, but he knew there was a small river running out into a sandy beach. So the first sandy beach we saw on the shoreline, we went in and anchored. It was about 7:00 P.M. September 12, 1938. Dad took the "go-ashore" and checked out the land and sure enough, it was Salmon Cove. The next day we went up Salmon Cove River in the small boat and cousins and uncles (the Peckhams from nearby Victoria) met us, helped unload the *F. Lydia* and we were all happy it was the end of the trip.

In time Philip Osmond moved to Lethbridge. He purchased an old school at Musgravetown, floated it to Lethbridge and rebuilt it as a family home. It is not known what happened to the faithful, solid craft which bore the family home. *F. Lydia*, which was not registered in Newfoundland or Canada, was likely sold or traded some time after and its eventual demise is obscure.

Philip was also a man who moved around a lot. He went back to Toronto for a period of time and later lived in Hare Bay, Gambo and Deer Lake. He spent his final years in Victoria, not far from Salmon Cove where his daughter Ivy resides today.

Toronto Star headline of voyage

Every Man for Himself

After making a few lumber trips to St. Pierre we fitted up, in the month of July 1935, for handline fishing up around the island of St. Paul and the Magdalens, but we were caught in a severe northeast storm on the eve of August 24, some ten miles north of St. Paul.

My radio warned us and I had listened over the radio until six o'clock. The gale was travelling at ninety miles per hour. I turned off the radio and prepared our little vessel as well as we could to meet the onslaught of this terrific storm which was now raging.

(John Marshall Fudge, 1970)

They didn't know how widespread the destruction was until afterwards, when it was all over.

Captain John Marshall Fudge, his four crew and the schooner *Geneva Ethel* were in the grip of an "August Gale," the tail end of a hurricane or tropical wind storm. These storms, which usually sweep southern latitudes in late summer, swing northward, but by the time they reach the maritime provinces, the force has dissipated to a gale. They still pack enough force to inflict disaster on ships and the men they carried. Although his schooner was over forty years old (built in Lockeport, Nova Scotia in 1894) Marshall, a veteran seaman and capable captain, knew the dangers and immediately prepared his little ship to survive the raging seas:

> We hove to under reef, riding sail and reef jumbo, and in the terrible sea were making good weather until the sheet clew broke in the riding sail. Then we ran before the storm while I put on a new clew on the sail, which took me about one hour.
>
> Unfortunately, this took up a lot of our space and brought us about ten miles closer to some bad rocks which lay to the leeward of us.

Marshall belonged to Belleoram; his crew was Fortune Bay seamen: Mate Joseph Burdock, Everett Fiander, William Tibbo and his brother Philip. They quickly repaired the sail and ran it up the mast. Slowly the schooner clawed away from the reef. Marshall, along with two other crew, went below for a few hours sleep but told the two on watch to call him at six o'clock. This is what he recalled:

> I woke about six-thirty, thinking that I heard a breaker roar. I rushed to the companionway, and behold, we were right in a roaring breaker. I at once tried to swing her off before the wind, but it was too late as the shoal wave started. I quickly realized that to take

it broadside was our only chance, as running off to
sea would swallow her up and she would go down
stern first. So I immediately brought her to and
hooked the strap over the wheel, every man for himself.

One man, William Tibbo, went up the rigging;
Everett Fiander clung to the foresheet, and Joseph
Burdock was in the cabin; while myself and Philip
(Tibbo), clung to the main peak halyards. The
breakers rose at least forty feet, rushing on to finish
her as it seemed certain death with my little craft full
broadside.

Waiting to meet the onslaught, I stood as cool as
I could be and prayed. We crested that raging mass
of water much easier than I imagined. When it was
about ten feet off I turned and took a tight grip on the
peak halyards, saying to the boy alongside on me,
'Hold on tight,' and then we were submerged for a
while.

Our little boat turned bottom up and slowly
came back on her side. When my head came above
water she was buried beneath the waves, and the
first that I saw looking forward was the top of her
bowsprit just coming up.

The sea had broken her jumbo boom and loos-
ened all the stops, and the terrific storm sent the
boom aloft. As soon as possible I fell down and took
the stops off the wheel and swung her off with the
help of the jumbo. So the next breaker did not reach
us to do any harm.

But poor Philip Tibbo was gone from our side.
As we were submerged quite a while we took in a
quantity of water. He may have smothered and let go
of his grip. We never saw his body.

The newspaper article of September 11, 1935, identifies
the crew member as Abraham Tibbo, not Philip Tibbo.
Captain Fudge, although writing from memory 20 years

after the accident, knew his crew and most likely writes accurately. Newspapers of the day often erred in reporting. Fudge was facing leeward when his head broke water. He immediately scanned the ocean and saw pieces of *Geneva Ethel*'s two dories, oil drums and other debris from the deck floating around, but did not see the young Tibbo man. Satisfied no more could be done, Fudge and his crew set out to save the schooner. Another crewman had a narrow escape from death, as Fudge recalled:

> In the meantime our little craft was full of water. This happened about 9:00 A.M. Sunday morning. About seven o'clock that evening we had her bailed out with buckets and the pumps working. All our food was spoiled, our stoves were smashed up; the forecastle stove broke from its lashings and went up and left the print of it in the deck. All our bed clothes were thrown down in the lee births.
>
> Joseph Burdock, who was down in the cabin settling things away, found himself hurtled in the lee berth, with the stove and radio and bedclothes from the other side jammed in on top of him. He was very nearly drowned there before he could move. In fact, he was in the worst place and I often wondered how he came out of it alive.
>
> All our gasoline and oil was gone. Booms and gaffs were broken, our bed clothes were soaked with water, and our dories were a floating wreck. We didn't break our fast from Saturday evening 5:00 P.M. until Monday evening 6:00 P.M. when we managed to get our stove together with wire and got a cup of coffee and dumplings.

According to the local paper, *Geneva Ethel* reported into Pushthrough. Fudge, in his book, claims he first went into St. Pierre and then proceeded home to Belleoram where he had the perturbing duty of reporting to Tibbo's family and loved ones that the young man had drowned on the voyage. He recalled the hardship it caused saying, "In all the ordeal of the August Gale 1935 stands out as one my terrible experiences and narrow escapes from drowning."

The loss of Philip Tibbo on *Geneva Ethel* was not the only casualty suffered around Newfoundland's shores during the August 1935 gale: the *Annie Young* of Ramea disappeared with eight crew – Skipper George Hayman, cook Bennie Hayman, John McDonald, John Warren, John Marks, all of Ramea and three men named Coley from Fox Island near Ramea.

On the other side of Newfoundland, *Carrie Evelyn*, sailing from Hant's Harbour to St. John's, was wrecked near Torbay. None of her four crew survived – Fred Mansfield of New Melbourne, Trinity Bay, age sixty; Ariel Green, age forty-two; brothers Elias, age thirty-two with two children, and Edgar Soper, around twenty and unmarried.

By Monday, August 26, reports trickled into St. John's of missing vessels, others driven ashore, many totally wrecked. Some were blown to sea, never to be seen again; others had men swept overboard to their death while handling wind-blown sails. The luckier schooners reported days later, heavily damaged, dismasted, stripped of sail and leaking.

Walter L with Captain Boutcher, his three brothers and another man named Wareham, all from Kingwell, Placentia Bay, came to grief. Some pieces of her wreckage drifted ashore at Pigeon Cove, twelve miles from Trepassey. About the same time, another unidentified vessel was reported sighted near Trepassey, on her beam ends, drifting around Cape Pine. Another, with only one mast, was seen off Powell's Head drifting helplessly.

The town most affected by the 1935 August Gale was Marystown. Captain Patrick Walsh, his two sons, aged eleven and twelve, and a crew of six were drowned in the vessel *Annie Anita*. The bodies of the captain and one of his sons were eventually found in the cabin of the wreck, located about a mile from St. Shotts, near the southern tip of the Avalon Peninsula.

On the same evening the schooner *Mary Bernice* from Marystown with Captain James Walsh, son of *Annie Anita's* master, was lost with four other crew. That wreck was towed into the settlement of Haystack, Placentia Bay. Another schooner missing was *J.R. Rodway*, Captain Ernest Walsh, a brother of the two captains lost. This vessel later turned up safely at St. Pierre.

The Titanic, the Majestic and the Antelope

Since the phenomenon of the 1997 hit movie *Titanic*, more people than ever, at least in the western hemisphere, have been captivated with *Titanic* trivia and still thirst, seemingly at an ever-increasing rate, for facts about the great ship operated by the renown White Star Line.

Newfoundland has its small claim to *Titanic* fame. Cape Race received messages from the liner as celebrities aboard the ship clamoured to be the first to send word to the United States via Newfoundland. When the wireless operator on the liner *Californian* tried to warn *Titanic* of the ice field, *Titanic's* operator, Jack Philips, gave his famous brush-off, "Shut up. I'm busy. I'm working Cape Race." In spring and early summer, icefields of the size and type that the great liner encountered can often be seen near Newfoundland's coasts.

On the night of April 14-15, 1912, the British liner, commanded by Captain Edward Smith, sank after striking ice approximately 500 kilometres (300 miles) southeast of Newfoundland. The disaster, which occurred on the ship's maiden voyage, claimed the lives of more than 1500 of the 2200 aboard.

By 1912, radio was in use on ships and *Titanic* sent out a distress signal received by Cape Race. *Californian* was equipped to receive the signal and was close enough that night to speed to the rescue, but it had only one radio operator and he, after receiving his brush-off from Philips, had gone to his cabin to sleep. There was no one on duty when the signal came in.

Because of the drama of the sinking, the number of lives lost, and the social position of many of the dead, the disaster revolutionized the rules governing sea travel. After 1912, all passenger ships were required to carry lifeboats with enough seats for everyone on board, lifeboat drills were to take place on every passage, and radio receivers were to be operating twenty-four hours a day.

In addition, in 1914 an International Ice Patrol was established and has been maintained ever since, to keep watch over the ice giants of the deep and especially so near the great drilling platforms (like Newfoundland's *Hibernia*) of the northwestern Atlantic.

Eighteen years previous to the loss of *Titanic*, the White Star ocean liner *Majestic* rammed and sank a Newfoundland ship. Local tradition has it Captain Edward Smith, who lost his life on *Titanic*, commanded *Majestic* at the time.

In July 1894, *Majestic* sped across the Atlantic delivering passengers from England to New York. On the night of July 30 while off southern Newfoundland, she encountered thick fog and slowed to half speed. In the inky darkness of

3:30 A.M., she sliced into a Burin schooner *Antelope*, drowning Gabriel Mitchell and fatally injuring William Woundy.

Antelope, a thirty-four ton three-dory banker, was owned by Burin's Bugden brothers: Reuben, age twenty; Benjamin, twenty-six; Fletcher, twenty-nine; Henry Philip, thirty-two; John, thirty-five and captain of the vessel; and Thomas, thirty-seven. It is not clear if all six owners were on this particular trip but certainly most of them were. In a quirk of fate, all Bugden brothers survived and were plucked from their schooner's wreckage by *Majestic*'s boat crew. Gabriel Mitchell's body was never found; William Woundy died in the liner's hospital room that night.

Majestic's passenger list shows boxer James J. Corbett, who in 1894,

EVENING Telegram
August 1893

BURIN BANKERS ARRIVED.

**How They Fared With the Fish
on the Banks.**

SEVERAL of the Burin bankers arrived from the Grand Banks the latter part of last week, and with good fares, too, when it is considered that they, for the greater part, only carry four and five dories. Here are their names and catches:—

The *Ocean Plough*, Vigus, master and owner, 300 quintals.

The *Bloodhound*, Benjamin Hollett, master, Bishop & Co., owners, 240 quintals.

The *Nereid*, Morgan Hollett, master, Robert Inkpen, owner, 190 quintals.

The *Hecla*, Kirby, master, George Inkpen, owner, 150 quintals.

The *Sammy Hick*, John Kirby, master, Bishop & Co., owners, 195 quintals.

The *Jessie*, Weir, master and owner, 160 quintals.

The *Antelope*, Bugden, master and owner, 160 quintals.

Lily, Goddard, master and owner, 100 quintals.

Happy-Go-Lucky, Roberts, master, Keech, owner, 100 quintals.

Artist, Vigus, owner, 150 quintals.

May Belle, Smith, master, Goddard, owner, 120 quintals.

And the *Bessum*, William Kirby, master, Bishop & Co., owners, 180 quintals.

The *Evening Telegram* in August 1893 lists Burin fishing vessels and their catches on the Grand Banks. The *Antelope*, Bugden, master and owner did well with 160 quintals.

was heavyweight champion of the world. Corbett, the first world champ under the Marquis of Queensbury rules (using gloves), was called to a room to view Woundy's body. According to story related by *Antelope's* crew when they returned to Burin, the boxer was amazed at the arm and upper body size and muscular definition of the tall fisherman. It is well-known that Newfoundland dory fishermen developed barrel chests and powerful arms from their many hours of rowing. Upon seeing Woundy's body, Corbett remarked, "He must have been a powerful man. I'm glad I didn't face him in the ring."

The mighty *Titantic*.

According to some local sources, Captain Edward Smith commanded *Majestic* in 1894, but this is incorrect. Since the tragedy of *Titanic*, several biographers have studied Smith's life in great detail: one comprehensive book, *The Man Who Sank Titanic: The Life and Times of Captain Edward Smith*, by Gary Cooper, states Smith commanded White Star's SS *Britannic* from July 1893 to January 1895, and in July of 1895 became captain of SS *Majestic*, staying with her until 1902. Such was his dedication and knowledge, he later captained the ill-fated *Titanic*. Clearly, Smith was not in charge of the *Majestic* in the *Antelope* collision; in fact, one newspaper account states Captain Parcell guided *Majestic* in 1894.

RUN DOWN BY THE BIG MAJESTIC.

The Schooner Antelope Sunk Off the Banks and Two, Lives Lost.

The Majestic of the White Star Line arrived yesterday with part of the crew of the fishing schooner Antelope of Burin, N. F., which she sank off the Banks on Monday morning. The crew of the Antelope consisted of eight men, six of whom were saved.

The Majestic had been running in a thick fog for two days before she struck the Antelope. While running at half speed and blowing her fog horn incessantly, shortly after 3:30 o'clock Monday morning, the forward watch reported a vessel right across the bows.

From the bridge full speed astern was immediately rung, and every effort was made to stop the steamship. The headway was so great, however, that before the reverse action of her screws could affect her she struck the schooner and cut clean through her, a little abaft her main hatch.

The shock to the huge Majestic was scarcely perceptible, but the cries of those

---

This is how the August 2, 1894 *New York Times* reported the collision at sea between White Star liner *Majestic* and the Burin schooner *Antelope*.

The surviving Bugden brothers were carried to New York, transported to Halifax, and thence to Burin. When they arrived home on August 15, they were heartily welcomed by residents. Although they displayed straw hats emblazoned with a White Star banner and wore White Star body sashes, they soon told the sad tale of the loss of *Antelope* and the death of two crewmates.

Bugden's Point, Burin. According to John Peacock, a relative of the Bugdens, the ship tied to the wharf may be the ill-fated *Antelope*.

Not to be confused with *Californian* (which unfortunately did not help rescue *Titanic's* survivors) is the transatlantic steamer *California*. The latter, of the Anchor line, cut down the Burin banker *Beatrice Vivian* on July 12, 1936. The schooner was lying to about twenty-five miles off Cape Race when *California* hit, putting the wooden craft to the bottom in minutes. Captain James Gosling and his twenty-five man crew all hailed from Burin and area. Unlike the wreck of *Antelope*, this time there was no loss of life.

Saved by a Horse

In the history of the North Atlantic, many ships are missing and reported lost with out a trace: freighters, tankers, schooners, yachts, steamships and clipper ships. The 10,000-ton USS *Cyclops* with 306 crew disappeared in March, 1918; the 9000-ton German freighter *Melanie Schulte* and the *Sao Paula*, a 20,000-ton Brazilian warship were just three of the many that have vanished without a trace.

Newfoundland vessels were no exception to unexplained disappearances in the North Atlantic. Dozens of its ships have never reported and are presumably lost with all crew: the Harbour Breton tern schooner *Grand Falls* in 1914; *Sydney Smith* of Carbonear; *Mina Swim* of Burin with 23 crew in 1917; and the banker *Alsatian* out of Grand Bank with 25 crew in 1935.

The Newfoundland ship which disappeared with the greatest loss of life was the SS *Erna*. According to reports, it had 51 people aboard. It carried its own 32 crew, most of whom were from St. John's; several passengers, included women and children; and the crew of a schooner, the *Aureola*. *Aureola*, owned by Bishop and Sons of St. John's, had been abandoned at sea, its men taken to Glasgow, Scotland, and were aboard the ill-fated *Erna* on its final voyage to Newfoundland.

Just as strange as these disappearances are the vessels that were found abandoned with the crews missing, the most famous of which was the *Mary Celeste* (often referred to as *Marie Celeste*, its actual name when launched) found by the brig *Die Gratia* in December 1872. Well provisioned and in good order, it was abandoned off the Azores for unknown reasons. No trace of Captain Benjamin Briggs, his wife, daughter and seven crewmen was ever found.

Discoveries of Newfoundland vessels abandoned in reasonably good shape with no trace of its crew are not as common. But there is at least one strange story of this occurrence. The *Nordica*, a two-masted schooner, became, for a brief period, one such vessel, found thirteen hundred miles from Boston in relatively sound condition with no one aboard to tell the tale. Even the beginning of this story – the background of *Nordica*'s purchase – deserves a second look.

Around the beginning of the twentieth century, two of the traditional bank fishing centres of North America,

Gloucester and St. Pierre, realized the advantages of beam trawlers powered not by sail but by steam engine. Just after the Great War, many of their schooners were replaced with trawlers.

In 1915, two businessmen from Grand Bank, John Ben (J.B.) Patten and William Forsey, seeing the success of steam trawlers in St. Pierre, were determined to try the new technology. Because of high demand, no trawler was available in Gloucester or St. Pierre, so the company sent J.B. Patten to England to buy one. He travelled there on one of his own schooners en route to Spain with a cargo of fish.

To his disappointment, the British Admiralty, in the midst of the German submarine blockade of World War I, would not release any vessels to be sold outside of England, and Patten returned home without a modern trawler.

What effects this might have had on the schooner fishing industry in Grand Bank, and along the south coast had he been able to bring a steam trawler to Newfoundland, is merely speculative. The era of dory banking and schooners might have been entirely different.

Patten then went to Lunenburg, Nova Scotia, with his money and his intentions to purchase a new vessel. There, he saw not one, but two schooners he liked, and unable to decide between them, he purchased both. *Lillian M. Richard* was put under the command of Captain John Thornhill and *Nordica* under Captain "Long" John Matthews. Built in 1912, at Allendale, Nova Scotia, the 123-ton *Nordica* had fished for three years out of Lunenburg, Nova Scotia, before Patten bought it.

Nordica made Newfoundland marine history when it was found drifting and abandoned, but practically intact, on October 26, 1920, at latitude 43.58 North, longitude 51.28 West. The schooner had sailed for Portugal with a cargo of fish, making the passage in twenty-one days, then headed for home with sand ballast. After leaving Oporto, *Nordica* bucked its way westward fighting heavy winds for more than a month. On board were Captain Thomas Payne, Seaman George Barnes of Grand Bank, four other Newfoundland seamen, and two Portuguese stowaways who had hidden on *Nordica* while it was docked in Oporto. Barnes of Grand Bank, in a short biography of his life on the sea written some years after, recalled his experiences on *Nordica*:

> I joined *Nordica*, owned by Patten and Forsey of Grand Bank, and captained by Thomas Payne from Curling, Bay of Islands.
> We sailed on August 2, 1920, for Portugal with a load of fish. We had a fine trip there, discharged, and took sand ballast for Grand Bank. All went well until September 20th, on the four to eight watch; we lost our rudder on the Grand Banks and had to leave her.
> Later, we got picked up by a Dutch ship, the *Wilfaro*, bound for New York. We were in New York for ten days. Then we came home by the *Glencoe*.

Barnes' account seemed to indicate the loss of the schooner on October 18, 1920, somewhere in the Western Ocean. Usually, vessels abandoned on the ocean were set afire so that the waterlogged hull, which could float for weeks barely awash in mid-ocean shipping lanes, and practically invisible by day or night would not pose a danger to other vessels. For some reason the derelict *Nordica* was not set afire.

In later years, neither Barnes nor anyone else satisfactorily explained why the crew left the ship so hastily; maybe there was no way to mend the broken rudder, or the captain, in consultation with his crew, perceived *Nordica* to be hopelessly adrift, and deemed it safer on the ocean in a small lifeboat than on an uncontrollable schooner.

Possibly some experienced crewman, seeing there was no way to guide the schooner into the shipping lanes, convinced the rest of his mates to row the lifeboat in that direction. Within the travelled routes, chances of rescue would be better. And indeed they were! Several hours after leaving *Nordica* behind, the lifeboat was sighted by a Dutch ship which picked up the eight men and carried them to New York.

To Captain J. L. Warren of the steamer *Western Comet,* who happened upon the abandoned *Nordica,* it must have reminded him of the brig *Mary Celeste,* that unsolved nautical enigma found 48 years before. Unlike the crew and passengers of *Mary Celeste,* who were never seen again, the men of *Nordica* were by this time, safely aboard *Wilfaro* and on their way to New York.

Western Comet was en route from Glasgow, Scotland, to Baltimore in October, 1920. When the lookout of *Western Comet* sighted the crewless craft at 9 A.M., he called Captain Warren to the bridge to observe the crazy meanderings of a schooner. In fact, the drifting boat may have meant disaster to the steamer had it not been discovered in the daytime, as the derelict careened and lurched across *Western Comet's* bow.

From the steamer, no sign of life could be observed and the schooner appeared neither damaged nor waterlogged, so Warren sent a boat and crew to investigate. One small sail had been set on the schooner, which moved it along a few knots in the light breeze.

The boat's crew had to row hard to catch her; as they passed near the stern, they read the name and port of registry: NORDICA, St. John's, Newfoundland. It was no easy task to manoeuvre near a moving schooner on the tossing

Atlantic, but *Nordica* was finally overtaken and two steel hawsers were made fast.

To the amazement of the boarding crew nothing appeared out of place except that the vessel had been hastily deserted with the foresail lying as it fell on the deck. Initial examination showed that *Nordica* had little solid food aboard – just fifteen to twenty cases of Spanish onions. In its tanks were 150 gallons of fresh drinking water; sails and rigging had no more wear and tear than could be normally expected on a sailing vessel on the high seas. There was no excessive amount of water in the bilges and all pumps were in good order. The logbook contained entries up to the hour of abandonment.

Grand Bank waterfront in the 1930s. The newly constructed "right of way" in the foreground leads from the head of the western pier to the fish stores of Samuel Harris Ltd. and Footes. The white heads centre are the bonneted beach women, waiting to go to work. The man on the rail (right) is the area where the Bait Depot is located today.

As the men of *Western Comet* made their way below deck, the apparent cause of trouble was discovered: the steering gear had two bolts sheared off, rendering the rudder useless.

Captain Warren figured the value of the schooner at about $15,000 and, seeing the potential for salvage monies, the steamer towed *Nordica* to Boston, arriving there on November 2. No difficulties were experienced towing the schooner, but the delay resulted in the steamer's coal supply being nearly exhausted. Stokers were down to sweeping the floor to gather enough fuel to reach Boston.

To the Boston newspapers, the salvage of a small Newfoundland schooner was no earthshaking event. *The Boston Globe* recorded the story on its third page with this heading:

THE BOSTON GLOBE—WEDNESDAY, NOVEMBER 3, 1920

ABANDONED VESSEL FOUND PLOWING SEAS

Nordica Picked Up Right in Steamship Track

Damage to Rudder Only Apparent Trouble—Towed to Boston

After sailing hundreds of miles without a hand at the helm the British fishing schooner Nordica was towed into the lower harbor early yesterday by the

The Boston Globe of November 3, 1920, reports the finding of an abandoned ship in mid-ocean apparently in good condition. The ship turned out to be the Grand Bank schooner *Nordica*.

Back in its home port of Grand Bank, there must have been mixed emotions when news from the Boston insurance and salvage companies arrived. Patten and Forsey were delighted to know their valuable banking vessel had been found intact. As soon as the owners made a cash settlement for salvage claims, *Nordica* could be taken home.

By a singular coincidence of the sea, *Nordica* was brought to Newfoundland by the crew of the Burin schooner *Ella C. Hollett*. That schooner, salt laden, had left Oporto on September 15, only a few hours behind *Nordica*. *Ella C. Hollett*, under the command of Captain Sydney "Copp" Hussey, had struck the same storm as *Nordica* encountered, and the *Ella C.* had to be abandoned. Unlike the *Nordica* however, it went to the bottom five hundred miles west of Oporto.

The steamer *County of Cardigan* rescued the crew from the sinking schooner, took them to Bermuda and they were thence shipped to Boston, just in time to be hired to take *Nordica* back home. This feat of the ocean and rescue of *Ella C. Hollett's* crew became a news feature in Newfoundland's *Daily News* (November 15, 1920) with the headlines WILL BRING DOWN NORDICA!

In the intervening time, while *Nordica* was being towed to Boston, Payne, Barnes, the other four crewmen, along with the two Portuguese stowaways, had arrived in St. John's from the United States on the Red Cross liner *Rosalind*. After a few days in St. John's awaiting connections with the SS *Glencoe*, the sailors returned to Grand Bank. The two stowaways were confined in the St. John's lockup until the Portuguese ambassador in Newfoundland at that time, R. F. Goodridge, lodged them in the Seaman's Institute. They were later returned to Portugal.

By the spring of 1921, *Nordica* resumed its fishing and foreign-going career, and in September, when the bank fishing season ended, loaded casks of dried fish destined for Greece. This time owners put the vessel under the command of an older and more experienced captain, George Tibbo, known in Grand Bank as 'Pluck' Tibbo, with his Grand Bank crew: Mate Neddie Hollett, Cook Daniel Gregory, Seamen Sammy Caines and Edgar Ralph; and Seaman George Barnes, who was a crewman when the schooner was abandoned less than a year previously. After its cargo was discharged at Greece, *Nordica* headed for the Strait of Gibraltar bound for Cadiz, Spain, to load salt for the return journey.

However, the gallant *Nordica* never made it out of the Mediterranean Sea. During a violent storm, the schooner went ashore on the eastern end of the island of Corsica, about three quarters of a mile south of Point d'Arco Tower. Fortunately for the Newfoundland seamen, the schooner drove ashore near a small village. The inhabitants who witnessed the grounding gathered on the shore to assist in the rescue. In the high seas it was impossible for them to heave a line or to wade out closer to the ship, but one Corsican thought on a novel method to effect a rescue.

Later, recounting the last hours of *Nordica* and the struggle of its distressed crew to leave the wrecked vessel, Captain Tibbo commended the heroism of the Corsicans to the newspapers:

> Our vessel was being pounded on the rocks and the sea was sweeping over the vessel in every direction, with death staring us in the face, when our dangerous position was seen by the natives of that sparsely populated island. Our position was desperate in that our lifeboat was full of water and could not be launched.
>
> Finally, a male resident of the island came along on horseback and urged his steed into the surf, with a line in his hand. He fought with his horse valiantly to reach us and, after five attempts, we caught the line he brought out.
>
> With considerable difficulty, we secured the line to the waterlogged lifeboat and after getting into it, though it was half full of water, we were pulled to shore and saved. *Nordica*, shortly after, went to pieces and sank, and we lost our personal effects but were treated kindly.
>
> From that place we were shipped to Marseilles, France, and from there to Paris, where we were cared for as are all seamen in distress. From Paris we went to London, England, and thence to Liverpool,

where we took a passage home on the steamer *Minnedosa.*

This was the final chapter for *Nordica* – abandoned in the Atlantic, salvaged, brought home, but finally wrecked a year later with the rescue of the crew brought about through the efforts of a horse.

Heroes at Lumsden Beach

If we wanted to save ourselves from this wreck we would have to get a line ashore. I asked one of the hands to go down in the cabin and bring up the heaving line. So I threw the line out and asked for slack when I threw it. Threw it and no, it went up along the stern and wouldn't drift in to shore. What are we going to do? Now, the rescuers are on the beach waiting for us to do something.

Mate Stewart Abbott, September 2001

F ive men were stranded eight hours on the wreck of the schooner *Alice M. Pike.* Steward Abbott and his shipmates could see the would-be rescuers standing along the beach, but they couldn't get out to the wreck and the stranded crew couldn't get to shore.

Alice M. Pike, a 65-ton schooner constructed in 1911 at McGill's shipyard at Shelburne, Nova Scotia, was owned for many years by St. John's business Harvey and Company. Harveys operated it out of Belleoram under Captain Benjamin Keeping. In the 1940s it was sold to the William Barbour business of Newtown, Bonavista Bay, and then Walter Collins of Carmanville bought the schooner. Other captains of the schooner were Wesbury Barbour and Cyril Kean.

In October 1950, Collins asked Captain Arch Blundon to take *Alice M.* to Lumsden to get a load of salt fish destined for St. John's. Abbott recalls the vessel's last voyage:

> I was home in Musgrave Harbour at this time and Captain Arch Blundon of Carmanville contacted me because he knew I knocked about on schooners. This was late October 1951, and he wanted me to go with him as mate to Lumsden to get a load of fish for Robbins' salt fish business.
>
> The other crewmen were Carl Pardy and Eugene Pardy, Musgrave Harbour and Uncle Abel Tulk, an older gentleman, from Carmanville.

On October 30, Captain Blundon anchored the schooner off Lumsden to prepare for loading the next day, but the wind came up a gale from the north-northeast. Although the *Alice M. Pike* had both anchors down, one of the chains broke and the schooner began to drift.

Blundon decided to hoist the jumbo and foresail and head for the smoothest place on the beach ahead, in the same place where the SS *Thackeray* had gone ashore in 1947. Mate Abbott knew the navigational dangers near Lumsden, for it had no real harbour, and had numerous rocks and reefs all around; besides it was exposed to northerly winds. He recalled:

> So we went in, anchored in Lumsden and we were just inside this crag of rocks. It was a beautiful evening, but you could see some weather was coming; being an old sailor you could almost smell the bad weather. The *Alice M.* had two engines, a 44-hp Kelvin and 88-hp Kelvin, so it had good power.
>
> While we there in the night, the wind started to breeze up. By and by it started to come heavy. The sea was just like a pan with suds, white water and foam – there was never a bit of blue sea nowhere.

By and by the skipper came to me. I must have been down in the cabin somewhere and he said, 'Come up. One of the chains broke.' This was nothing strange because the chain might have had a weak link. The best chain is only as strong as the weakest link. The links could be all rusted out, see.

We had to get the foresail up and the jumbo – the jumbo does the work in sheering the boat off. Now right there to the stern of the schooner – and the wind was northeaster blowing us right into it – was big bunch of rocks. No lives could be saved if we went in there because we could have struck that and down comes the spars and off come the planks.

We couldn't get out to sea for the wind was right in the cove.

In the evening of the next day, October 31, Captain Blundon decided the best thing to do was to let the chain go, when the crew raised the sails, in hopes of gently beaching the craft. It was his intention to reach one of the sandy beaches and perhaps refloat the vessel later.

By this time quite a crowd had gathered on the shore-line watching the hoisting of the sails and sensing the *Alice M. Pike* would run aground. While the crew worked at unshackling a link, Mate Stewart Abbott stood to the wheel:

When the chain let go, someone called 'Starboard,' so I hove it in and I can see the schooner now in my mind as it forced in toward the beach. And when *Alice M.* struck the beach, the wheel come out of my hands. I was stood up with the wheel like this, see. When it struck the wheel went right back and I caught myself on the edge of the cabin.

The wheel and rudder shaft backed up and went right out its casing. The screw wheel come right out of it threads, the cogged wood, and tore it out my hands, whippo.

Alice M. Pike grounded about two hundred feet from shore. Breakers hit the vessel, roared on past and crashed down on the beach. There was no way to get the lifeboat off the stranded ship nor was it possible to launch a lifeboat or dory from the shore.

The five crew spent the night huddled in the cabin, peering occasionally toward the land and wondering if the winds would pitch down. When daylight came there was no let-up in the gale force winds. The *Alice M* shuddered with every comber that broke across its bulwarks. Blundon couldn't help but wonder, How long would it last with the pounding? If they couldn't get in with this wind, what would happen if it intensified?

In the morning the crew tried throwing a line out in hope it would drift to shore. Mate Abbott recalled the anxious moments:

> We were eight hours stood up in the cabin with the seas roaring down, rolling down over just the same as if you were on a beach with a big sea all coming down over your head. We were holding on.
>
> Daylight came. We saw the men on shore coming over with a dory – pulling a dory along the sand. They had to keep back on the beach because of the big sea coming in and they couldn't launch it.
>
> Since the rope wouldn't float in to shore, I said to one fellow, 'Go down in the cabin, get a piece of canvas and bring it up.' There's always plenty of old material lying around. I got the canvas, twisted it and tied it. I took the heaving line and I put it on like that like you would a balloon. When I threw it out, the wind caught it, and it didn't sink. So 'twas like a kite on top of the water.
>
> 'Boys,' I said, 'It's going to do it. If it doesn't go up around the head of the schooner, we'll do it because once the float gets in the tide that will take it ashore anyway.

Nearly everybody in Lumsden was there on the beach.

Slowly the canvas drifted in, as the crew slacked the heaving line after it. But a float will only go so far before the rope attached to it becomes too heavy and the float stops drifting. Someone on shore would have to walk out to grab the line. Abbott remembered:

There were two fellows – they were in the army in WWII – Clyde Gibbons and Caleb "Key" Gray from Lumsden who walked out nearly to their necks and grabbed the line with the piece of canvas.

They tied the big rope on, attached it to the dory, and we pulled the dory out to us. Two of the older fellows got aboard, and the people ashore pulled in the dory to shore. Then we pulled it back and the next trip the skipper and another man went. According as they reached shore, the kind-hearted people of Lumsden took them on to a house to get dried off and warmed.

I was left until last. By this time I was getting hungry and thirsty, so I wondered if there was something to drink in the galley. I went up forward and there wasn't much seawater only a couple of feet under the deck. I edged over to where we kept the food, picked out a tin of milk and drank it out of the can.

Since I was last off, I took all the rope and threw it in the head of the dory and made a motion to the shore I was coming. When the dory hit the gravel, one fellow guided me up the beach and he took me to a house – one of the Goodyear families.

And that was the end of the *Alice M. Pike*, an abandoned wreck on Lumsden beach.

The next day the crew went down to the shore to view the wrecked ship. Wind and surf still battered the shoreline and they realized there was no way to salvage the stranded schooner. They stayed in Lumsden nearly a week and when the coastal boat came, they took a passage to their homes in Carmanville and Musgrave Harbour. Abbott said, "The schooner was still beating and banging up, full of water with the spars and masts all down. There were no goods aboard to salvage because we didn't get to load the fish."

People of Lumsden recall that stormy October day. Elmore Gibbons remembered that Clyde Gibbons walked

When *Alice M. Pike* was owned by E.J. Green, Winterton, a group of people paused from their busy day's work for a photo aboard the schooner: from left to right, Alex House (at the wheel), unknown, local teacher Eric Parrott (white white shirt and pipe), Captain James Seaward (with hands on legs), Nick Green, Winterton, (far right with arm on barrel). Middle row, (l-r), unknown, unknown, Edward Seaward (with high black hair). Back row standing near mast, Robert Seaward.

out into the surf to help the crew get off. Clyde was nearly swept off his feet and almost drowned. Others reached him and pulled him back, but he had grabbed the rope from the stranded schooner. Many young fellows, including Elmore and Rex Gibbons, who were on the beach that day, had a hand in pulling in the ropes with the dory attached.

For years the remains of *Alice M. Pike* could be seen about halfway down Lumsden South beach, but it has since disappeared.

Alice M. Pike (above at Winterton) was commanded by several captains over the years: Ben Keeping of Belleoram; Wes Barbour of Newtown, Arch Blundon of Carmanville and Cyril Kean. At one period James Seaward of New Perlican commanded the schooner. The land, left, is Western Point and the photo was possibly taken in 1930 from the head of E.J. Green's wharf.

Race to St. Pierre

In the 1930s, as the era of the sailing schooner along the South Coast of Newfoundland drew to a close, owners found that profitable voyages or charters for foreign-going vessels were getting more and more difficult to find. This was due in part to the Great Depression, or as it was known in Newfoundland, the "Dirty Thirties," when prices for fish, like most exported goods, fell to low levels. Many merchants had tied up or sold their vessels; other schooner owners collected and transported salt dry fish destined for Europe from wherever they could find a cargo around Newfoundland or St. Pierre.

In the spring of 1932, Harris Export Company of Grand Bank consigned *General Wood* to take fish from St. Pierre to France. To make the round trip profitable and complete, exporters in St. Pierre also ordered her to Bordeaux, France, for a shipment of whisky and rum for St. Pierre wholesalers. Repeal of prohibition in the United States was still over a year away, and St. Pierre liquor purchased by rum-runners fetched a high price on the American east coast.

General Wood, considered to be a fast sailer and a good sail carrier, was a tern schooner or three-master and netted one hundred fifty-nine tons. She had been built at the Arthur Story yards, Essex, Massachusetts, in November, 1920. As was his custom for naming schooners in honour of British generals, Grand Bank merchant Samuel Harris christened this vessel for Brigadier General Leonard Wood (1860-1924), who led British troops in World War One.

Steve Will Forsey commanded *General Wood* with his Grand Bank crew of Ben Snook, mate, and three sailors: Fred Smith, Len White and Joe English. His cook was William Baker, who had sailed with Forsey on several transatlantic crossings, but this voyage was one Baker would not easily forget.

With favourable winds, the voyage from St. Pierre to Europe was quick and uneventful. After the fish was discharged, *General Wood* headed for Bordeaux, the wine capital of France, located sixty miles up the Gironde River. After a week-long delay, Captain Forsey finally engaged a tug to tow them upriver. When the liquor cargo was aboard, Wood waited again for a tow back to the Bay of Biscay where the journey home would begin.

At the mouth of the river, much to the chagrin of Captain Forsey, a wild storm was brewing with winds that eventually rose to eighty or ninety miles per hour from the west-northwest. This spate of inclement weather forced Forsey to anchor *General Wood*, in company with several other westward-bound vessels, just off the coast of France.

In the course of the delay, Forsey fell into a conversation with the captain of a French brigantine anchored nearby. When both captains realized that they had the same destination, St. Pierre, a friendly wager was agreed upon – a case of France's finest whisky to the vessel that first dropped anchor in St. Pierre. Both captains shook hands to seal the bet and went back to their respective ships. As soon as wind direction changed and the storm settled, both vessels hauled up anchors and set sail for the French Islands. Both vessels would soon separate on the vast expanses of the North Atlantic.

Cook William Baker of *General Wood* may, or may not have been aware of the wager at the time, but, undoubtedly he was as eager to get home as the rest of his shipmates. That March morning just as *General Wood* had weighed anchor, Baker had the duty, as cook, to carry what he termed, "the dog basket" back to the after cabin. The dog basket, a sailor's term for a small wooden food tray, contained breakfast for the captain. As he came up the companionway from the galley and set foot on deck, an enormous wave passed over the schooner, carried away the stovepipe, split open a companionway door and swept the cook off his feet.

Hurtled across the deck, head over heels, Baker had nothing to grab to stop his fall. Most three-masters built in the Maritimes had a straight, or flush, deck, but *General Wood*, designed at Essex, had a two-level deck. It was into this wooden projection that the cook struck his legs, an impact which splintered his right kneecap. In that split second he was carried along by the white water toward the rail. Barely conscious from his tumble, he desperately tried to grab a line, rigging, rail or any fixed object and save himself. But the comber carried him over the side and into the ocean.

All too often during wild Atlantic storms, Newfoundland sailors were washed overboard, their names became a forgotten statistic, entered on obscure logbooks as "lost at sea." Only a tremendous set of circumstances that morning combined to save Baker's life.

The sea in that area was not bitterly cold, as it was in mid-ocean, but warmed somewhat by the Gulf Stream. Hypothermia, the cold water killer, did not paralyse his limbs and sap his strength; yet the shock of hitting the water helped him regain his senses long enough to scream for help. Like many Newfoundland sailors, he couldn't swim a stroke. With a broken right kneecap, even his ability to keep himself afloat was limited.

As fate would have it, all the crew were on deck that morning, preparing the vessel for her journey home. Mate Ben Snook, from his position on the port side, foresaw the potential danger to the cook as he opened the galley door and reacted instinctively. He saw his helpless shipmate wash across the deck and was ready to help in an instant.

The mate spotted a loose rope and coiled it for a throw. He knew he would have only one chance to make his aim true; time wouldn't permit a second trial. The struggling man had already been in the water a minute and was twenty or twenty-five feet away from *General Wood*. True to the mark, as if the hand of God had guided it, the lifeline fell close enough so that Baker grabbed it, found the strength to hold on and was pulled safely aboard.

In pain, bruised and broken, Baker lay in bunk for the entire journey with nothing to relieve his agony. In those days, aspirins and pain killers were virtually unknown on a Newfoundland schooner. All that could be offered to relieve pain and suffering was a hot tarry oakum compress placed on his knee.

From France to Newfoundland, *General Wood* battled contrary winds and storms, taking forty days to complete a voyage usually made in three weeks. No doubt Captain Steve Will Forsey must have been elated he had not had a man drowned on the journey.

Upon arrival in St. Pierre, the captain saw the French brigantine in port ahead of him. She had been there for a week. As *General Wood*'s captain honoured his wager, he found it hard to swallow his pride and admit defeat. Grudgingly, Forsey admitted that, even with his cook laid up, which in effect left the tern shorthanded in adverse weather, he still should have given the French vessel a better run for her whisky.

General Wood had to remain in St. Pierre a week to offload her cargo of liquor to French dealers. Baker was transferred to Tom Murphy's schooner *Dauntless*, headed for Grand Bank. At Grand Bank he was carried to his residence on Ralph Street. Doctor John Burke, the resident physician, came to assess the knee. He lanced the swollen skin and blood spurted out – as his wife Susan remembered – to splatter the ceiling and wall. Baker was transferred to the Banker's Hospital where the doctor reset his shattered kneecap as best he could.

Although he recovered from his injuries and in later years, as an able seaman climbed the rigging to the top mast hundreds of times, William Baker always carried the scar inflicted on *General Wood* in March, 1932.

In 1942 the aging *General Wood* had outlived her usefulness as an overseas trader. She was sold to a business woman in Bermuda, and the registry transferred out of Newfoundland. When she sailed out of Grand Bank harbour, the last tern schooner was gone forever from that port. She took with her memories of danger and adventure on the treacherous ocean highways.

Tern schooner *General Wood* was built at Essex, Massachusetts, in 1920 for Samuel Harris. In 1932 it was manned by Captain Steve Will Forsey, Ben Snook, Fred Smith, William Baker, Len White and Joseph English. From 1918 to the 1940 fish merchant Harris owned 17 tern schooners, many of them named after WWI Generals.

Three Short Sentences

George was well over eighty years of age and straight as a whip when I talked to him in his home on Church Street. On his faded photo showing the town's soccer team of long ago, he stands tall in the back row, his height suggesting a defender, or as he said, a fullback. George had a ready smile and was delighted to recount his seafaring days as he sat in his high-backed chair, talked, showed me his diary and asked only anonymity in return.

In his early years he fished from a dory on one of the dozens of banking schooners operating out of his home town. After some time at that, he handled sail on tern schooners. When the era of sail passed, he worked on steamers and Canadian freighters until he retired from the sea.

I knew from previous conversations, George had been a crew member on the schooner *Jean McKay*, where disaster had struck, and wanting to learn how that ship sank and the details of the loss at sea, I asked him about his experiences.

George had kept a diary – a journal about his life at sea. It was just a cheap notebook stored in a chocolate box along with other papers, documents, and photos. It was yellowed foolscap containing entries written long ago in blunt heavy pencil. It was not a daily account, but contained snippets of information about significant personal happenings experienced in a long sea career; entries pencilled months, and sometimes years after the event.

It was amazing really that such a notebook had survived at all considering the number of life-threatening situations George had endured: ship fires, severe ocean storms, crew mates washed overboard or lost while dory fishing, the inevitable wreck, sinking vessels and rescue. Three times he had abandoned ship in various areas of the North Atlantic when his battered schooners, seams opened during violent throes of mid-ocean gales, slowly sank beneath him.

To George's way of thinking, surviving storms on gale-wracked hulks was just another job hazard – something to be faced, and when over, it was back to the sea on another ship if work were readily available. Many young men – family men – he knew had disappeared over the years, all victims of the treacherous Atlantic. Patras, Oporto, Cadiz, Pernambuco, Turks Island were exotic ports of call, but the journeys there or back claimed Newfoundland ships and men by the score.

The diary – there it was, none the worse for wear, considering. It was no secret: George proudly showed his words to anyone interested in reading it and listening to his stories. No doubt family members had seen it often, friends occasionally and strangers, like me, rarely. His entry on the *Jean McKay* was pencilled in as three short sentences, so I asked him if he could tell me more about that misadventure. Here is George's story, slightly edited for clarity. He wrote:

(Diary entry) That fall I signed on the Jean McKay for a trip across.

Built in 1918 at Shelburne, Nova Scotia, the 194-ton *Jean McKay* was owned in Grand Bank by Patten's, a local business that cured and exported salt cod. For twelve years, this tern, or three-master in local terms, had plied the waters between Europe, the West Indies and Newfoundland. In September 1930, the *Jean McKay*, with a fish cargo loaded at Harbour Buffett, Placentia Bay, headed for Oporto. On the return journey, deeply laden with salt, a typical mid-Atlantic storm opened her seams. For four days the schooner wallowed deeper and deeper as water poured into her bilges faster than the pumps could keep it out.

Captain Cyril Squires ordered his crew of five men to work the pumps and to keep a sharp lookout for a passing ship in the hope of rescue. Then, on October 16 (as verified by the October 21, 1930 edition of the *Daily News*) that ship appeared. But George's memories are not of the trauma of getting plucked off a sinking ship just before it went under; rather, the unforgettable conditions aboard the rescue ship.

The Jean McKay had to be abandoned at sea.

George voiced it this way:

The Captain had ordered lookouts and signs, so we went up in the rigging to the masthead and put up distress signals. Several steamers sighted us and saw our signal fires, but turned away. By this time our schooner was down quite a bit in the sea. Although we had lots of drinking water, most food was gone. Rationed bread, a slice or two a day; biscuits; several sacks of Spanish onions and that was about it. By the time we were rescued, everyone was ravenous hungry and dog-tired from manning the pumps continuously for four days.

We were picked up by a passing ship...

This night a freighter came along that saw our signal fire and took us off the sinking J*ean McKay*. I can't remember her name, but it was a British steamer about 5000 ton coming west from out of the Far East, China, perhaps and had passed through the Suez Canal and Gibraltar. Let me tell you she had a strange cargo and that knowledge came as a surprise to all of us Newfoundlanders.

The cook put food on the table for us. Although we were starving – without a solid meal for over a week – we wouldn't touch it. It was like blood. It seemed to be a pudding, about the size of an ordinary water bucket, and it was red, blood red in colour. That was all was on the table beside our tea. We wouldn't eat it; afraid of what it was and waited till the next day to eat.

...and taken to...

Anyway our rescue ship had 300 Oriental passengers, all men, going to the United States as labourers. For the most part, they stayed below in the hot, overcrowded steerage, but we sometimes saw them on deck in good weather, standing and lying around, passing time.

Not long after we were called up to the bridge by the captain of the steamer.

Pointing at me, the captain said, `You broke path for the coolies.'

I was kind of thunderstruck at first. `Sir, what do you mean broke path?'

`In the companionway you stepped aside to allow coolies to pass,' he said. He waited a few minutes to allow that to sink in. `I guess you noticed that all the officers on this ship wear side arms.'

I had. Each had a small holstered gun attached to his belt.

The captain stared the crew of the *Jean McKay* in the eyes. `There are only a few of us Englishmen controlling this ship and 300 of them cooped up in a hold where there's only room for fifty and they're not fed well. If they see any sign of weakness, it would be a simple matter for the coolies to take this ship, throw all of us overboard, and no one would know what became of us. We're outnumbered about a hundred to one.'

The meaning of the captain's words came clear to me then. Of course we treated all people with courtesy and dignity; it's something that's born and bred in us, but that time respect got us in trouble.

Not long after, we struck another Atlantic storm which sent mountainous waves across the decks of the freighter. On deck there had been several cages of wild animals captured in Africa – birds, monkeys, other small creatures destined for American zoos. A cage containing six or seven monkeys broke open in the gale scattering monkeys everywhere. Two or three were washed overboard and the rest managed to escape to the ship's steel stays and riggings, wireless cables, and so on in the masts.

The caretaker, a Frenchman whose job was to ensure the safety of creatures, paid us to climb the masts to try and get them back. The prospect of a few dollars made us risk the danger, but the terrified animals were too wild in that storm to let anyone get near them. They bit, clawed and clambered out of reach, so we had to come down and wait for better weather.

By the next day, there were no monkeys left in the riggings. During the night in the cold wind and heavy seas, they must have perished for we never saw them again.

...Curacao where arrangements were made for our transportation home.

After that incident the weather changed for the better. The captain had no further problems with his various passengers; it was smooth sailing until we reached the island of Curacao in the West Indies. From there arrangements were made for our passage to New York and then home.

The tern schooner *Jean McKay* anchored in an European port, probably loading salt. On October 16, 1930, it sank in mid-Atlantic, but the crew was plucked off in time.

Words pencilled in a modest diary. What would happen to them? What would happen to the stories between the lines? Like the passing of the tall ships, the ranks of schoonermen grow thinner each day and many of their heroic tales of wreck and rescue have gone from our knowledge. As George finished his story and put his diary away, I could only marvel at and admire this unassuming seaman. He had been snatched from a watery grave and carried to safety by a strange and unforgettable rescue ship and had recorded the event in three short sentences – brief entries that left more unsaid than said.

War at Sea

A Battle of the Atlantic

All throughout the war at sea between 1914 and 1918, Newfoundland ships continued to take salt fish to Europe. War-starved Portugal and Spain generated good prices for Newfoundland's top export. But to get the fish there, many ships ran a deadly gauntlet between storms and enemy submarines and cruisers. Several Newfoundland schooners were intercepted and sunk during the Great War. However, the nemesis in this story of the sea is the age-old enemy, the stormy Atlantic and the cold winds of February.

Although the fish carrier *Albert A. Young* finished its career on the bottom on the bottom of the Atlantic in 1918, there was no official report of its sinking in local newspapers. Perhaps shipping casualties from German subs made better newspaper copy, or censorship of wartime losses limited specific details of ship sinking. At this time, too, another great shipping tragedy was deemed more newsworthy – the wreck of the SS *Florizel*, the recovery of bodies, and the subsequent enquiry into the loss. The Red Cross passenger liner wrecked near Renews on February 26, 1918. Ninety-four passengers and crew drowned. The government enquiry into how and why this tragedy happened got under way almost immediately and lasted for over a month.

At any rate, the wreck of *Albert A. Young* comes directly from an account from its Captain, Clarence F. Dodman, a man with only one leg, but nevertheless a knowledgeable and veteran sea captain, well-versed in navigating the Atlantic. The 92-ton *Albert A. Young*, built in Lunenburg in 1912, was owned by George M. Barr of St. John's and, although its crew is identified, their place of residence is not given. Since the schooner was based out of St. John's, it is likely Dodman, Mate Ronald Moore, Cook Pat Ryan, and Seamen Pat Clancey, Joe Critchton and Dan Keefe were from St. John's or the Avalon region.

The fact that the Atlantic was patrolled by enemy ships didn't deter Newfoundland's hardy sailors from delivering, or at least attempting to deliver, products to Europe. *Albert A. Young* left St. John's on January 17, 1918, well-laden with fish for Corunna, Spain. Between these two points was nearly three thousand miles of winter ocean.

From the outset the schooner met a succession of gales, snow alternating with hail and rain. Seas were high. This spate of annoying weather dogged Dodman and his crew until they were 500 miles east of Newfoundland; then conditions took a turn for the worse. Hurricanes out of west-northwest and south-southwest roiled up some tremendous seas which buffeted the ship day and night.

About January 20, Dodman noticed the schooner was leaking at an alarming rate and ordered the men to the pumps. But despite their best efforts, no perceptible reduction could be seen in the level of water in the hold. Dodman decided to jettison some cargo; thus the lightened ship would make better weather. It was nearly impossible to work the deck and open the hatches, so they had to chop through the forecastle bulk heading to get into the hold.

Armful by armful, the fish was passed up and thrown overboard. This had the desired effect. *Albert A. Young* rode the seas and fought adverse winds much better, but only for a short time. Seas now began to break across the deck, putting everyone's life in jeopardy. One wave took the dory from its lashings, broke it into kindling wood, and swept much of it overboard. There was no let-up at the pumps for the crew, now reaching the point of exhaustion.

Albert A. Young gradually sank lower, the cargo of dry fish became soaked as spray constantly went into the companionway and the specter of death stared the men in the face. Dodman decided to run his ship under bare poles and did so for 60 miles until the schooner became unmanageable in the seas. One wave beat in the heads of the water casks on deck; except one. At 4:00 A.M. another sea breached the deck and carried the anchor and chains aft; this mass of iron tore off the cabin. The crutch for the main boom was broken and the sea tore away the bulwarks on the port and starboard side.

Albert A. Young was now waterlogged and couldn't sail even if the weather improved. When dawn broke on February 1, another tremendous sea swept the second boat out of the chocks and damaged the stem of the schooner. But an hour or so later, a steamer could be seen about two miles away bearing east-northeast and the crew ran signals of distress up the mast. Much to the amazement of the fatigued crew, it sailed somewhat closer and stayed within viewing distance of the sinking schooner, but shortly after continued on its course.

From that point weather improved somewhat and this lasted until February 6, although there was no let-up at the pumps. It was a case of get the water out or have the schooner sink beneath their feet.

On the sixth, *Albert A. Young* met a convoy of eight ships which could do nothing to help the doomed vessel. The crew knew the convoy, all British merchant ships, had no armed protection against enemy subs and, in their direct and swift course would not stop.

Not long after these two disappointing encounters, the crew saw smoke on the horizon. Captain Dodman with his spyglass informed the crew it was a large ship, and in an hour or two would cross the schooner's path. When the ship saw the distress signals it altered direction and ranged down within hailing distance. It was a British destroyer, eastbound. When the crew of *Albert A. Young* hailed the ship, they said their schooner was waterlogged and in danger of sinking. Lieutenant G. Nailer, R.N., decided to attempt the rescue as soon as possible.

There was no way Nailer could have his sailors launch a lifeboat in the high seas. He then had lifelines shot or thrown to the wallowing schooner. The first line to reach *Albert A. Young* was tied around seaman Pat Ryan, who jumped overboard to be hauled through the water to the destroyer. As Ryan was pulled up over the side and onto the deck, he was struck by a shackle on the heaving line, which opened a large gash on his head. The destroyer's doctor immediately took him to sick bay for medical attention.

Nailer saw that this means of lifesaving was too dangerous and placed the destroyer to within a few feet of *Albert A. Young*; so close it struck the schooner's jib-boom and that in turn broke some railing on the destroyer, and smashed a lifeboat, causing about $500 worth of damage to the British ship.

The remaining five Newfoundland seamen had to jump from the swaying sheer poles (a wooden or iron bar attached to the shrouds just above the deck railing) or from the rigging to the destroyer. Each one managed to land on the deck of the warship and not in the Atlantic. Dodman, who was less agile than the other with his one leg, was the last to jump. He left behind his nautical instruments and, like the others, all his personal effects and extra clothes.

When Captain Dodman jumped from his sinking schooner, *Albert A. Young* was nearly underwater; in fact, there was only one strake of plank, or covering board, showing above water. Nailer, seeing the derelict could become a floating hazard to navigation, fired five explosive shells into the wreck. Four found the mark, with the first hitting below water line. The gallant schooner soon nodded its final farewell and slipped beneath the Atlantic.

The crew of the destroyer treated the Newfoundland seamen with great hospitality and landed them in Liverpool, England. All, except Pat Clancey, who found work in Liverpool, left for home and reached St. John's on March 7, 1918.

"This War No Good, Jack"

Throughout the 1939-45 Battle of the Atlantic, many Newfoundland fish merchants continued to send their schooners laden with cargoes of salt cod to ports in Greece and Portugal. It was dangerous times. Yet, the captains often went without the aid of convoy protection for the simple reason that the sail- or motor-driven schooner could not keep up the pace.

Convoys were established to keep open the lifeline to the United Kingdom, but in the Atlantic the Allies still lost 2,603 merchant ships totalling 13.5 million tons, say Terry Hughes and John Costello in their 1977 book *The Battle of the Atlantic*. So, being in a convoy was no guarantee of safety, and the freighters and warship escorts tended to leave smaller craft behind, especially during frequent Atlantic storms when the ships would lose contact with each other and would scatter over a wide area.

Four crossings were made by *Robert Max*, a 173-ton wooden schooner owned in Grand Bank, on Newfoundland's south coast. She set sail on her fifth wartime crossing in late July 1941, under Captain Harry Thomasen with a crew of Newfoundland merchant seamen: Gordon Hollett, Luke Rogers, Alex Banfield, John Douglas and Sam Pardy.

When Captain John Thornhill bought part shares in this 180-ton vessel in 1929 in Nova Scotia, he renamed it *Robert Max* for his two sons who had died of diphtheria some years before. According to Nova Scotian tradition, the 9 letters in her name would prove unlucky, but this omen was unfounded; she had a long and productive career, until intercepted by a German sub in August 1941.

August 4 dawned beautifully and clear. The schooner was 1100 miles from Newfoundland and off the Portuguese coast. A little after midday a German submarine surfaced nearby, fired one warning shot across the stem, one over the masts, and ordered the boat to heave to. Under orders from *U-boat 126* Commander Ernst Bauer, Thomasen and two crewmen rowed over while the other three Newfoundlanders sailed the schooner up into the wind and then lowered the jib, a small sail. This allowed *Robert Max* to drift slowly down near and past the sub.

"From where we were, we could see her flag with the swastika on it," seaman Sam Pardy recalled years later. "We kept jogging around and after a while we saw the skipper and the two men coming in the dory. They hollered, 'Heave off the lifeboat. We only got ten minutes!' They rowed up around the port side and tied the dory on against the forward rigging."

Captain Thomasen later related (in Andrew Horwood's *Captain Harry Thomasen Forty Years at Sea*) that on board the sub he was interrogated about *Robert Max*'s cargo and destination. Although the schooner was not armed, the Germans decided to sink her, for in their view, she carried food for Allied nations. The crew of *Robert Max* were given ten minutes to gather personal belongings and move away.

The first four shots were aimed at the two spare barrels of gas and kerosene strapped against the cabin. Almost immediately these exploded and burst into flame. Several shells plowed into the engine room near the foremast putting this section of the schooner afire. As a final show of bravado, the German gunners took aim at the forerigging, and cut the halyards, causing the foresails to fall. Next the mainmast and mainsail received several rounds.

Under a barrage of 28 shots, *Robert Max* went under, but as if unwilling to resign herself to the deeps, the schooner sank only until she reached her mastheads, near the cross trees. From several yards away in the open lifeboat, the six Newfoundland seamen watched her for about fifteen minutes. Finally she gave her farewell nod and disappeared.

Each man bent to the oars to pull away from the lonesome scene, where only an hour before, their home and refuge on the sea had sailed. As seaman Pardy recalled:

> This was not a nice experience to go through, but then we rowed away. The submarine came up again alongside, took us aboard and we went up talking to the captain and some sailors. The inside was hot. The sub's crew all had their underwear and pants rolled up to the thighs and were barefooted.
>
> Captain Thomasen went to the conning tower. I was up three steps and put my hand on the gun that fired at us. I had to take it off quick it was so hot where they had used the shots.

The German commander gave them a course to the coast of Portugal and, in a gesture of humanity, offered to attach a steel cable to the lifeboat and tow the captain and crew toward the nearest land. He added a word of caution: if enemy planes approached while they towed the lifeboat, the sub would have to make an emergency dive and possibly take the lifeboat with her.

Thomasen refused. Then the Germans offered to tie on a rope instead of a wire cable – a rope could be chopped quickly. But fearing an attack upon the submarine by Allied planes or ships, the captain took his chances in an open lifeboat that he knew was well-manned and provisioned. Most likely the good weather and favourable wind would push them to the coast. He organized the six crew members into shifts for rowing and keeping watch. Pardy recalled:

> We came 297 miles in seventy-two hours aided by oars, a small sail and a good wind by night. Our hands got shiny on the last of it from rowing, and bailing which was necessary because the lifeboat hadn't been in the water for a year. We'd have turns: John Douglas, Gord Hollett and I sitting on the bottom of the boat where we'd bail out water. When we'd get up our rubbers would be full of water. It wasn't very comfortable – six men in a small boat and their hands sore.
>
> The course they gave us wasn't right. It was a long ways out. We were 700 miles from Portugal, but there's three islands out in the ocean, the Azores. Well, we got to the southernmost one that was about 90 miles long.

The men saw the purple smudge of Santa Maria at 1:30 P.M. on August 6. Its mountains could be seen from quite a distance away. It was not until twelve hours later they reached and anchored off its lee shore. Thomasen, Pardy and the other men had found the port of Ponto Delgado on the island of Santa Maria, Azores. "We had 120 fathoms of buoy line and an anchor with us, and we put that overboard and lay down to rest. I made a cigarette out of some Jumbo tobacco we had. I tore a leaf out of the old man's *Belcher's Almanac* and made a smoke out of that."

As daylight broke on August 7, they were seen by a local fisherman who guided them through the rocks to safety of the beach. Their odyssey was over.

Pardy reflected on the German sailors he had encountered – young men like himself caught in a drama they had no control over: "On board the submarine, you know, there was this German about my age and size. He said to me, 'This war no good, Jack. No good for you, no good for me.'"

In the Line of Duty

The HMS *Laurentic*. The name and details of the marine mishap of this great ocean liner probably doesn't mean as much today as that of the tragic tale of *Titanic*. Both ship names end in IC which indicates the two transoceanic liners are somehow related. They were built at the Harland & Wolff yards in Belfast and were owned by the renowned White Star Line. Both ships came to violent ends in the North Atlantic.

When *Titanic* went down in 1912, there were no Newfoundland passengers or crew, but on *Laurentic*, sixteen Newfoundlanders died. Today one can find their names inscribed on World War One monuments and memorial stones located all over the island. Three of the sixteen were from the Burin Peninsula: George A. Brinton, son of Herbert and Ellen Brinton, Port au Bras; Leslie E. Walters, son of George and Mary Walters of Lamaline; and Samuel Mayo

Hooper, son of James and Frances Jane Mayo Hooper of Creston South. Samuel joined the Royal Navy at age 20, trained on the HMS *Briton* (ex *Calypso*) in St. John's and left for Europe in September 1915. As a Royal Navy Reservist (RNR) he fought for King and Country and, like several other young men of Newfoundland and Labrador, was assigned to HMS *Laurentic*.

Although designed and built as a luxury passenger liner, the outbreak of World War I in 1914 brought different duties for *Laurentic*. It was requisitioned as a troopship capable of carrying 1800 soldiers. With the installation of eight 6-inch guns, the ship was converted into an Armed Merchant Cruiser; *Laurentic*'s final war voyage was fast approaching.

In order to pay America for munitions and armaments for the Great War, many vessels carried valuable cargoes to the United States and *Laurentic* was no exception. In the bitter cold of January 1917, it departed Liverpool, stopped at Ireland and left for Halifax, carrying 45 ton of gold bullion – 3211 ingots each weighing forty pounds (about 300 million in today's values). Also aboard was its compliment of 460 officers, crew and military passengers, including about 20 Newfoundland reservists, some coming home on leave.

In the evening of January 25, *Laurentic* left Buncanna, Ireland. At 6:00 P.M., while sailing around Fanad Head, it struck two mines laid several days before by the mine-laying German submarine, U-80. What happened next is best described by *Laurentic*'s Captain Reginald A. Norton:

> I was on the bridge when a violent explosion occurred abreast the foremast on the port side. It was followed 20 seconds later by a similar explosion abreast the port side engine room. Nothing was seen in the water prior to the explosion. The ship was steaming at full speed ahead with no lights going.

> I ordered full speed astern, fired rockets and
> gave orders to turn out boats. I tried to send a wire-
> less call for help, but found the second explosion
> had stopped the dynamo.

In one stroke the blast adjacent the engine room left *Laurentic* totally without power and lights; the pumps couldn't operate and the lifeboats had to be launched in the dark, a daunting prospect. Norton tried to call the engine room, but the inter-ship telephones were silent. Nor could the ship send an SOS – the batteries were damaged or destroyed in the blast. Norton asked his Yeoman to signal Fanad Head on the lamp.

The ship was alone in the black of evening and sinking. Captain Norton could see some of the port side lifeboats had been swung out and lowered down to the choppy seas. He grabbed his megaphone and shouted for those aboard to wait, but in the howling wind and the pitch dark they drifted off to the leeward.

Norton remembered there were men down below locked up in cells, probably crew who had been rowdy the night before. He said to the navigator, Lieutenant Walker, "There are four chaps below deck in cells. Get them out." Walker could not find the keys, and had to get shipwright Harrington to chop the doors down with an axe. Another lieutenant reported the engine room was full of water and the eight officers and all the men on duty there had been killed.

The starboard lifeboats were sent away with orders to steer for Fanad Head. The last remaining lifeboat was lowered level with D deck to await the captain. As the last man to leave, Captain Norton made a final look around and was satisfied there was no one alive left aboard. He slid down a rope and into the lifeboat, so overloaded it was in danger of being swamped. *Laurentic* carried seventeen boats with a total capacity for 800 people; all boats got away except three, although not all were fully loaded.

They pulled for Fanad Head, Ireland, about a mile or so away, but in the wind, heavy seas, intense cold and darkness, most lifeboats didn't make it. They were carried westward, away from land. The captain's boat was luckier; the crew made a sea anchor and it drifted less distance. At the official enquiry Captain Norton said:

> At last I entered the waiting lifeboat, bumping dangerously alongside the sinking ship, but owing to the darkness I did not actually see *Laurentic* sink. Possibly some crew were killed in the engine room, but I am not sure of that as no survivors are left of the men on watch. I know all got out from the stokehold. The survivors suffered much in the open boats, due to exposure in the coldness of the night. My boat was almost full of water when we were picked up by a trawler the next morning.

Within four hours, trawlers – often called the Royal Navy's "Mosquito Fleet" – went out to the wreck site. Of the 14 lifeboats, six were found with men still alive; the others were either not found or were located with all occupants dead from exposure. In total, 12 officers and 114 sailors were saved. Three hundred and forty-four crew and passengers were lost. Many bodies drifted in on the Irish shore or on offshore islands.

Within days, rumours around St. John's and the rest of Newfoundland said that *Laurentic* had been sunk with great loss of life. Official word came on January 31 from Anthony MacDermott, Commander of the Royal Navy in Newfoundland, who was stationed on board HMS *Briton* in St. John's harbour:

...A telegraphic report has been received from the
Admiralty that the names of 16 seamen of the
Newfoundland RNR do not appear in the list of survivors of the *Laurentic* and they are missing,
believed killed. A list of the men with their next of
kin and addresses is attached.

Included in the list were Brinton, Walters and Samuel
Hooper. Other boys ranged from the width and breadth of
Newfoundland. Although no complete roster of survivors
was located, it is believed about five or six
Newfoundlanders lived through the ordeal, including E.J.
Greene of Heart's Content.

Newfoundland Seamen lost on HMS *Laurentic*, January 25, 1917

Alexander Ayles, son of James and Mary Ayles, Temperance Lane, Bonavista
James J. Benoit, son of Alice Benoit, Stephenville Crossing
Leslie Brinston, wife Susie, Old Shop, Trinity Bay
George A. Brinton, son of Herbert and Ellen Brinton, Port au Bras, Burin
Erastus Cumby, son of late George and late Hannah Cumby, Hopeall, Trinity Bay
Ephriam Freake, son of Mary Freake, Joe Batt's Arm
Eldred Gosse, son of Robert Gosse, Long Beach, Random, Eldred's wife was
Elizabeth Gosse of Queen's Cove
Samuel M. Hooper
Laurence Murphy, son of James Murphy, Conception Harbour
William Puddicombe, brother of Mrs. Patience Curran, Cook's Harbour
Frederick Randell, son of Elizabeth Randell, Fogo
Simeon Rogers, wife Bertha Rogers, 176 Water Street West, St. John's
Luke Smith, wife Isabella Smith, Butter Cove, Random, Trinity Bay
John C. Tucker, wife Mary A. Tucker, Ship Cove, Port-de-Grave
Leslie E. Walters, son of George and Mary Walters, Lamaline
Wallace Young, mother Ellen, Flat Bay, St. George's

A month later, the Court of the Admiralty concluded the
Captain and his officers had acted prudently and were not to
blame for the disaster. The loss of *Laurentic* and so many lives
was tragic but, as far as the British Government was concerned, the gold bullion had to be brought up quickly. A
recovery team went to work immediately. Divers spent sev-

eral years getting the gold, using explosives to blast their way through the ship's hull. The job was finished in 1924, although 22 ingots were unaccounted for and were probably lost through blasting or when the weakened ship was torn apart by storms. Today the "Big L" is a much-frequented spot for amateur and professional divers; some search for lost gold and others dive for sentimental reasons.

) A YEAR.

BAY ROBERTS, NFL. FRIDAY, FEBRUARY 16, 1917.

Laurentic Sunk by Mine

About 260 men were lost in the sinking of the auxiliary cruiser Laurentic, many of them having been killed by the explosion of a mine, which sent the former White Star Liner to the bottom, says a

The Bay Roberts newspaper *The Guardian* carried the tragic tale of *Laurentic*.

Samuel M. Hooper's body was found in one of the lifeboats and he is interred in the Upper Fahan Churchyard in County Donegal, Ireland. His native marker today stands proudly in front of the Marystown Town Hall on grounds that are pleasant and inviting, unlike the elements on that cold January night of 1917 when *Laurentic* went down.

There is another, albeit unofficial, story of Samuel. His parents knew he was coming home on leave, and one evening, his mother while having tea saw him through the window. His father James went out to check and saw nothing. James knew young Samuel liked horses and went to the barn where Samuel's brother Stephen kept his horse.

Samuel was there. To the father's surprise, he was sitting on the edge of the hayloft, dressed in his sailor's suit, but silent and sad. When his father spoke, the young man fell from the hayloft to the floor and vanished from sight. James Hooper knew then his son would never come home and, shortly after, received the news Samuel had died in the line of duty on HMS *Laurentic*.

Samuel Mayo Hooper, George Brinton and Leslie Walters are remembered on the Marystown, Burin and Lamaline War Memorials.

Samuel Hooper in his naval uniform.

HMS *Laurentic*, built as transatlantic liner in 1908, sunk as an armed Merchant Cruiser in 1917. *Laurentic* was 550 feet long and nearly 15,000 gross ton; in comparison, *Titanic* was nearly 900 feet long at 46,000 gross ton. *Laurentic*'s triple-expansion turbine engines gave it extra speed and in 1911 it set a record for a passenger ship on a journey from Liverpool to Montreal and back.

Murder and Riot

The Unsolved Mystery of George's Island

Everyone loves a good mystery. Was Anastasia Romanov executed with the rest of her family in 1917? Whatever happened to the crew of the *Mary Celeste?* When and under what circumstances did the steamer *Beverley* disappear with 23 Newfoundlanders aboard in early 1923? Not as well-known as these mysteries, but nevertheless just as puzzling, is the mysterious death of several men on George's Island in 1876.

George's Island, located in the southeastern side of Groswater Bay on the northern coast of Labrador, was once a favoured fishing station visited by fishermen of mainland Labrador and Newfoundland. Off the cove near the entrance to the main settlement, also called George's Island, are numerous reefs and underwater rocks; in fact the shoals near the island were the preferred grounds of several Newfoundland fishermen, including Captain Nathan Norman of Brigus.

One of the more dangerous ledges is called "The Reef of Norman's Woe," most likely named for some mishap to one of Norman's ships. Eventually any permanent livyers on George's Island re-located, but the island was still in use as a summer settlement at least up to 1981.

George's Island was, according to the Newfoundland and Labrador Encyclopedia, "a colourful and much-frequented" location and in the fall of 1876, shipwreck and murder became part of the island mosaic.

The Hudson Bay Company schooner *Walrus* left Rigolet, Labrador, on October 15, 1876, sailing for Grady to load more fish. From there it would sail to Montreal with a cargo of salmon, trout, fish oil and other fish products. There was a strong headwind and a heavy sea, so the captain decided to anchor for the night off George's Island.

By the next day the wind increased to gale force and it looked as if *Walrus* would be driven onto one of many reefs off the island. The captain and his crew launched the small boat over the side and attempted to land on George's Island.

Alas, the age-old story of wreck and ruin prevailed. The boat upset in the surf and all, with the exception of one man, drowned. In the mishap, the bottom of the boat struck a rock which put a hole in the craft. *Walrus*, unaffected by the gale, stayed firmly anchored at its original spot where the crew left it.

The solitary survivor (who remains unidentified) stayed in the general vicinity for five days, then decided he would have to go back aboard the schooner. He plugged the holes in the boat with his jacket, rowed out to the *Walrus* and climbed up over the side. As soon as he slipped or unfastened the anchor cables, he was not able to handle the vessel and *Walrus* ran aground at Black Island, Groswater Bay, a total wreck.

Perhaps the story should end here, for that was the tale of the loss of *Walrus* as told by the survivor to fishermen of the Labrador coast. If the saga had ended well for him, perhaps he was rescued and given transportation to his home.

But, as it turned out, the fishermen of George's Island saw things differently. Instead of being drowned in the unfortunate circumstances of leaving a ship, the captain and his crew were cruelly murdered. That same fall a crew of "green fish" catchers, i.e. those who split and salted codfish, then shipped it salt bulk or undried, went to George's Island looking for bait. They had some reason to land there and, to their horror, found lying on the strand, the bodies of three decapitated men. But there was no sign of their skulls.

Their clothes and limbs were all intact. The fishermen could see at a glance that the condition of the men had not been caused by the sea. Furthermore, the bodies were well beyond the high water mark. Searching around, they found, about sixty yards farther west, another body. On this one, the head was still attached, but had been cleft, as with an ax, in four pieces.

Suspicions aroused, the fishermen made a wider search and found two large canvas tents, probably made from a ship's sail. Judging from the size of the tents and the trampled ground around them, they figured the tents had been erected by more than one man.

There was nothing else to be seen or learned and the men covered the bodies with sand. They walked over to the opposite side of the George's Island and located Mr. Job Williams who lived on the island. The fishermen related all that they had just discovered.

At once Williams went to the murder site and found that the story told him was correct in every horrible detail. Taking the canvas of the tents with him, Williams went to Fish Cove, a small fishing station on the mainland, located on southern entrance to Groswater Bay.

At Fish Cove there resided Thomas Pottle who, it seems, had several men hired as fishermen who also prepared his fish for market. After Williams related the particulars of this mysterious affair, Pottle, with his son Samuel and some of his crew, visited George's Island. They too found the bodies in the position and condition exactly as had been described.

Pottle also discovered in a small crevice in the rock near the spot where one of the tents had been erected, several interesting and equally mysterious items – a number of half-decayed books and papers, as well as a woman's photograph. Who it was, they had no idea.

To Pottle and his men, this seemed to prove rather conclusively that *Walrus'* small boat had not upset in the surf and drowned nearly all occupants – as alleged by *Walrus'* sole survivor. They could only reason the captain and three men had been murdered. At no time did anyone discover the missing heads of three.

Aerial view of George's Island, Labrador, the scene of mysterious murders.

After Pottle's group re-interred the bodies in the sand well above the high water mark, they walled the makeshift grave with stone. They left George's Island with its ghastly occupants and returned to their homes at Fish Cove.

Eventually the migratory fishermen carried the gruesome account to Conception Bay where it was published in the papers of the day. In the nineteenth century, the law as we know it today did not exist on the remote shores and on the isolated offshore islands. There was no police investigation. To this day it is not known what motivated someone to not only murder four crew of the schooner *Walrus*, but to remove the heads of three. And what of the survivor? Who was he and did he ever pay for his crime?

Colourful deeds, to be sure, all on George's Island many years ago.

Oh Brother, Passion and Anger: Murder in Small Town Newfoundland

Edward Follett pulled up his dory on the beach and threw a few sticks of firewood on the shore. He slung a coil of rope over his back and walked toward his home. It was Saturday, a little after 4:00 P.M. on May 30, 1891. A man walked out from behind an old store and stood in front of Edward with a double barrel shotgun aimed at his chest. Edward knew the man. It was his younger brother, James. "Jim, don't you cock the gun," Edward pleaded.

A single shot echoed along the beach and through the quiet town of Grand Beach. Edward cried, "Oh, look!"

and fell back, face up. Sixty-eight tiny but lethal shot wounds did the work. The dead man lay on the beach somewhere between the high and low tide marks and within sight of his own home. James immediately went toward his house, put away his gun, and walked back and forth in the front yard, wringing his hands and saying, "He did wrong and I did right."

Murder at any time is a repugnant act. When committed by a brother – fratricide – everyone asks what motive the murderer had to do the deed. Greed? Anger? Passion? What would drive someone to commit cold-blooded murder in a small village where everyone knew each other and where the two brothers, Edward and James Follett, had grown up together?

Grand Beach lies about twelve miles east of Grand Bank near the toe of the Burin Peninsula. In 1891 it was busy with a lucrative fish trade, chiefly lobster, herring and cod. There were eight homes in Grand Beach, several fishing sheds and stores. Most property owners had a back garden with vegetables, sheep or cow pastures with a small enclosure for the livestock. Some families had a farm or 'cow-house' set back in the countryside. The surrounding country was wooded and game abounded; in fact, the brothers Follett knew where wild geese nested in summer and collected eggs. A single road or path, less than a mile long, winds its way between the beach and the row of dwellings along the shore. Grand Beach, at this time, had no church or school.

The fishing trade brought its own business. Near the gut, or the entrance to the shallow harbour stood a lobster factory owned by a Nova Scotian business and managed by Isaac Collins Harding. He had employed four local people to can the lobster as it was supplied by fishermen from the area. It was in the act of delivering lobsters to foreign markets that Edward Follett, later murder victim, had been involved in a tragic shipwreck on the vessel *Ortolan*. On October 5, 1877, the schooner wrecked on the island of Langlade. Five drowned, but Edward was one of eight survivors. (See the book *Between Sea and Sky* for details of this wreck.)

Herring, a prized and abundant bait fish, abounded in Fortune Bay in the late 1800s. Some fishermen had made a living selling the bait to the French until the Bait Act of 1887 forbade the trade. Grand Beach was centrally located between the bottom of Fortune Bay, where most herring schooled, and the French islands of St. Pierre-Miquelon where good prices could be had for herring. At that time herring were plentiful near Grand Beach.

To help curb the illegal selling of herring bait and to convince the people to use the bait to fish themselves rather than deplete the stocks for foreigners, the Newfoundland government assigned police to various towns in Fortune Bay. On May 9, 1891, Constable Maurice Murphy of Carbonear was assigned to Grand Beach for a month. He soon found he had extra duties in a domestic dispute and, on May 30, murder most foul.

This deed, when the facts came out in the St. John's courtroom in June 1891, revealed the answer – a love triangle. Everyone in Grand Beach knew what was going on and what led James to commit the ultimate act of crime.

For the sake of propriety we shall call James Follett's betrothed, 'Sis.' In Newfoundland, it is more than a nickname, it was and still is a term of endearment, although there was lots of love lost between James Follett and Sis. It seems as if every time James was out fishing, or travelled the 12 miles to Grand Bank to get supplies or went into the woods to cut firewood or to gather food for his children, Sis and Edward got together. James often questioned his wife about this and, according to friends and relatives, she always denied it. Sis claimed her husband was excessively jealous and was always trying to force her into a lie.

As far as James Follett was concerned he was sure of the sexual inclinations of his wife. For anyone who was interested he could point out the place in the stable where she and his brother once lay together. On another occasion two of his children ran into the house to say their mother and Edward were in the store together.

James said:

> One day I went fishing and I felt so bad over my wife's conduct that I thought I would drown myself. I had to give up fishing on account of the things that were going on. For some time back we had been continually arguing and rowing. I was so troubled about my wife that from the first of May I could not sleep or work.
>
> On the day I came out of the woods, having been in search of wild goose eggs, I saw a dory on the shore, and I thought it was going to carry off my wife, as she had previously threatened to leave me. I went in the room and I said to her, 'Sis, are you going to lead a better life than this?'

This was his last discussion of the matter. In happy times, James was a quiet man. He was of average height, with dark hair, dark complexion and, by his own admission, had little in the way of book learning or education. Most neighbours knew the forty-year-old man as a good provider for his children, but as for what premeditated him to murder his brother who was four years older than James, that was for the court to decide.

An hour or so after his dire deed on the beach, James Follett was arrested in his home by Constable Murphy.

Murphy warned James not to say anything that could be used as evidence against him and the prisoner made no attempt to resist arrest or to deny what he had done.

About eight o'clock on the evening of the murder, some men from a Burin schooner anchored off the harbour and a Grand Beach man named Rideout carried Edward's body to a store, erected a platform of several logs and laid the body on it. In time it was interred in the local graveyard.

James was taken to Grand Bank and put in jail to await the arrival from St. John's of Judge Daniel W. Prowse, acting as an investigator for the criminal act. At Grand Bank on June 2, Prowse questioned Follett before proceeding to the scene of the tragedy. Prowse felt a more comprehensive port mortem had to be taken of the body and he had it exhumed. He also questioned several people and subpoenaed them as witnesses. Before leaving Grand Beach, he drew a plan of the houses and various structures in the town.

On June 3, the group left Grand Bank for Placentia on the Bait Protection ship *Lady Glover*; thence by train to St. John's. There were several people with Judge Prowse who were all to play a part in the trial: the prisoner; Isaac Collins Harding; Constable Murphy; the resident doctor at Grand Bank, Allan Macdonald; Doctor Philip Thomas Hubert; Grand Bank's stipendiary magistrate George Simms, and Abraham Seeley.

In addition, Prowse brought with him witnesses for the crown: James and Edward's sister, Maria Hiscock; their neice, Catherine Hiscock; Edward's widow, Susan (Rideout) Follett; and Rebecca Jane Guilliard. James and Edward's mother was asked to travel to St. John's as witness, but did not, claiming as a mother to both she could not give impartial statements. Her age and lengthy travel also prevented her from going to St. John's.

The preliminary trial began on June 8, 1891, in the courthouse in St. John's. Presiding over the proceedings were Chief Justice Robert J. Pinsent and Justice Joseph Ignatius Little. Perhaps James Follett could not have found a more competent person to represent him in the whole colony of Newfoundland – Sir James S. Winter. James Spearman Winter was born in Lamaline, across the tip of the Burin Peninsula from Grand Beach. Winter studied law after he finished his schooling, practiced in St. John's, and was first elected to Newfoundland's House of Assembly in 1873. He eventually became the leader of the Conservative Party and then Prime Minister of Newfoundland in 1897. Throughout his political career he continued to practice law.

Now he defended what seemed to be a clear case of murder, but Winter was determined to prove his client was provoked into the deed. Rage and passion forced James Follett to shoot his brother. Perhaps the verdict could be reduced from capital murder, which is premeditated or planned, to manslaughter, which is committed without malice but in an act of passion or rage.

Monday Morning, June 15: Twelve jurors from St. John's were selected and sworn in: Enoch Fry, William Noseworthy, James Stevens, Eli Dwyer, Patrick McGrath, George Payne, Joseph Pearcy, Stewart Noel, John Tobin, Timothy Minnute, Charles Lester and Michael Merry.

Crown prosecutor, Robert J. Kent, Queen's Counselor, called his first witness, Judge Daniel W. Prowse. He entered as evidence his map or plan of Grand Beach and pointed out various dwellings – those of the prisoner, the murdered man, witnesses, the stores and the lobster factory.

On cross-examination by Sir J.S. Winter, Prowse stated he had been sent to the Burin Peninsula specifically to investigate the case. When he reached Grand Bank he interviewed four witnesses, then proceeded to Grand Beach. Prowse asked around to determine the extent of the dispute between Edward, James and 'Sis' Follett. "I made enquiries as to the truth of the suspicion the prisoner held regarding his wife and brother, and elicited all the facts I could. There were frequent quarrels between the accused and his wife. The policeman had been called in twice."

Catherine Hiscock, the seventeen-year-old niece of both men, was called to the stand as the second witness. Hers would be the most credible evidence. Those in the courthouse could not help but remark that this was an intelligent witness who looked refined, mature and seemed older than 17. Her remarks of what happened on May 30 were clear and given in a sound, logical manner.

After saying she knew everyone who lived in Grand Beach, she pointed out the accused in court saying he was her Uncle Jim, her mother's brother. On the day of the murder she had prepared dinner at twelve o'clock, cleaned up and went into the loft of the new house her father was building nearby. She was knitting near the window and could see out over the harbour from the window.

> I saw Edward throwing wood on the beach...I then saw Uncle Jim point the gun and fire at him. I heard the report of the gun. They were about the length of this courtroom apart. Uncle Edward fell backwards on the beach and I heard Edward say, 'Oh look' just before the gun was fired. Uncle Jim ran toward his house after he fired the gun. I ran downstairs and began to screech when I saw this and then bawled for the policeman. I saw the body of Uncle Edward on the

beach and afterwards in his house, dead, on the Monday following.

On the cross-examination, Winter merely asked her age and asked if she had seen or spoken to James Follett prior to the murder. She replied he had been at her father's house the day before, but she was not there and didn't know why Uncle Jim visited. The court adjourned for the morning.

Monday Afternoon, June 15: Maria Hiscock was sworn in, stating she was Catherine Hiscock's mother, a sister of the prisoner and the deceased and that she was on good terms with both. Her description of the shooting was similar to Catherine's. On cross-examination by Winter, Maria explained that Edward had married Susan (Rideout) Guillard two and a half years previously. Susan was first married to Edward Guillard (who had been ill for many years and subsequently moved to Grand Bank where he died) and both had five children, all living in Grand Bank. Edward and Susan also had five children – three born before Guillard passed away and two born after Edward Follett and Susan were wed.

Upon questioning, Maria spoke of the tempestuous relationship between James and Sis Follett:

> For some years there was trouble between James and his wife. About a fortnight ago I saw her raging terribly, cursing and swearing at her husband, beating her fists against the table. James told her to speak quietly and sit down. That was the only quarrel I saw between them. It was three or four weeks before this trouble occurred. I thought he was out of his mind he was saying so much trash.
>
> I heard him say he couldn't live with his wife she was getting so bad. He gave up working and didn't do anything at all, so it preyed on his mind. Others

remarked on it as well as me. I went into his house to try to pacify him, to get the trouble out of his mind, but he said he could not banish it. I tried to talk to him, but he got too violent and I walked away. He never told me the cause of his trouble, but I understood that it was jealousy. It was Edward he was jealous of.

When he gave up working he used to walk about with his hands behind his back. He came out of the country one day crying to his mother that Edward had his wife carried away. That was the Wednesday before the shooting.

Susan Follett, Edward's widow, took the stand. Her observations of the killing agreed with Maria's and Catherine's. Upon questioned by the defense lawyer, Susan explained the family relationships. She had previously been married to Guillard for 20 years, but after his death married Edward. "I was born in Burin," stated Susan, "and I know nothing about any trouble between Edward and James. I was on good terms with James and his wife. We have no quarrel, but we left off visiting each other. Edward and James were not as good friends as the other brothers. The cause of it was jealousy. Before James was married, his wife was in the family way and he blamed Edward for it."

On a brief re-direct from Crown lawyer Kent, Susan identified her dead husband's clothes and then explained, upon questioning, that James had never complained to her of her late husband's extra-martial affairs. James had been at their home in April, but with no quarrel.

Next to bear witness was 15-year-old Rebecca Jane Guillard, born to Susan and Edward Follett before her step-father, Edward Guillard, passed away. On that fateful Saturday, Rebecca had been employed carrying herring to a field owned by Charles Follett. She had seen James some time before four o'clock pacing back and forth in his house. Winter's line of questioning to Rebecca attempted to establish the over-wrought state of mind of James Follett. "I saw James," she said, "on different days and in different places walking about before the killing and thought it strange he was doing nothing. I didn't speak to anyone about it. I didn't know anything about the quarrels between James and Edward or between James and his wife."

Monday's final witness was Abraham Seeley. His occupation was given as a carpenter, but on the evening of the murder he was on a lobster smack near Grand Beach harbour. He heard the shot and was one of the first on the scene, helping to carry the body to a shed. There was doubt cast on some testimony of Seeley who had heard a shot, but had seen nothing only a dead body. He had also listened to the utterances and speeches of the accused as he was being transported to Grand Bank in the evening of May 30. Much of Seeley's evidence was not admissible.

Tuesday Morning, June 16: The police constable, Maurice Murphy, testified he was assigned to Grand Beach as part of the Bait Act protection service. On the evening of May 30, he was just outside Grand Beach on a schooner as it prepared to go to Burin. About that time, 1:30 P.M., he saw James walking up and down on the road. Later in the afternoon Murphy said his vessel was further down the Grand Beach Barrisway – a half mile away from the scene of the crime – when the shot rang out.

> Two men came down and called out to me. Seeley and I went along the beach till we came to the body. There were spots of blood on the face and blood

oozing through his garments. I felt the forehead and found the body was dead.

I made enquires and as a result went to James Follett's house. He was walking up and down, but had nothing in his hand...we went into his house and I took a gun that was there and gave it to a special constable named Garland. I told James he was under arrest for killing his brother Edward and warned if he said anything in my presence it could be used against him. He was handcuffed and taken by boat to Grand Bank. On board the schooner were myself, two special officers, Seeley, the master of the schooner and his boy.

On board the boat, even though I cautioned him again, he said, 'I have been troubled with my brother this last 12 or 13 years and now I'm clear of him. I took the gun and went out to my brother and told him to confess to me or else I'd shoot him. I pointed the gun and pulled the trigger.' Seeley also listened to all this.

According to Murphy's statement, James had been to Grand Bank on May 20 to purchase powder and shot. When Murphy confiscated the gun, he knew from experience it had been fired recently. "When I saw the gun, I saw that the nipple had the flash from the cap still on it and that is a certain sign of recent firing."

When the guards and prisoner arrived in Grand Bank that night, the accused was placed in the local jail. On Monday morning, June 1, Constable Murphy returned to Grand Beach with Magistrate George Simms; Reverend George J. Bond, the Methodist clergyman; Doctor Allan Macdonald, and Doctor Hubert. By then Edward's body was in his house where the doctors removed some shot from under the skin.

Murphy also testified that he had been called to James' house twice before; the first time he and his wife were arguing. James was asking his wife to confess her flirtations to him. She spoke up to say she wasn't going to do it because he wanted her to tell lies.

On Murphy's second visit the two had been fighting. "She had struck him with a stick. He came in and began to cry. I used to meet James every day and we bid each other the time of day. I knew Edward better than James."

Defence lawyer Winter asked what the general feeling was in town on the defendant. The constable had heard the neighbours say the man and wife were leading a desperate life. When Murphy had talked to the accused and took his gun in the evening of May 30, James had said, 'Come into the stable and I'll show what I fired it for.' In the stable he pointed to marks or depressions in the sawdust where Edward and his wife had their illicit rendevous while James was gone to Grand Bank.

Then when re-examined by the Queen's Councillor, Murphy said the impressions in the sawdust could have been made by anyone.

Dr. Allan Macdonald's evidence was of the examination of the body, where the wounds were, and which of the swan shot, especially those in the chest and lungs, were fatal.

Tuesday Afternoon, June 16: To Winter's questions, Doctor Macdonald testified he had no reason to believe the prisoner's mental condition was in any way impaired.

Magistrate George Simms' stay on the witness stand was brief. He had gone into the prisoner's cell in Grand Bank on Sunday, May 31, to formally charge him with murder. James said to Simms, "I am glad I did it and ought to have done it two years ago." On Tuesday Simms and Rev. Bond visited Follett again. The accused then felt sorry he had shot his brother and wished he had left his wife before.

Doctor Hubert, who graduated with his medical degree from McGill, was in Grand Bank in May 1891, working with Dr. Macdonald. His testimony was mainly of the post mortem in Grand Beach. In a footnote of the tragic, Hubert, born in Harbour Breton and the son of Philip Hubert, JP, contracted diphtheria while in St. John's. Only twenty-four, he died on July 17, a little over a month after the trial.

The final witness called was Isaac Collins Harding. In May 1891, he was working for the second summer as manager of the lobster factory in Grand Beach. He heard the shot, looked and saw a man stagger and fall. On the cross examination, Harding said he, with the help of four Burin men from a schooner, helped carry the body to the shed. A man from Grand Beach named Rideout prepared the logs to lay the body on. He had also seen the prisoner walking about for some days, but did not speak to James or Edward at that time.

Wednesday Morning, June 17: When the court opened at 10:00 A.M., Justice Robert Pinsent informed Winter the accused could make a statement to the jury.

James Follett left the dock, walked slowly to the stand and spoke in a low, soft voice:

> About four years ago I saw my wife go into the cowhouse of the forest farm in the company with my brother, Edward Follett. At dinner time we had words over the matter on which my wife ran away. After a short time she came back again. Two years ago, on April 19, they went there again and I caught them in the act of criminal intercourse.
>
> I never saw or heard anything else until May 25 of this year, but my child told me on that day they were in the store together. We had a row over this matter, but she told me she would not change her course of conduct.

James gave other examples of his wife's infidelity and his increasing torment over the matter, concluding with the events of May 30, 1891. On that morning he had been in the woods in search of wild goose eggs and, upon returning, saw a dory on the shore and thought it was there to take away Sis. That caused another argument which boiled over when Sis said she would not change her ways. James had said as he ran down the stairs, "I will stop you from doing it," and walked out the door with the shotgun.

All witnesses had been called. Sir James S. Winter addressed the jury to summarize the case on behalf of the accused. He said the case was attended with peculiar difficulties. "The Crown," he concluded, "had not conducted the case properly and the strict course of law and justice had not been followed." Winter then spoke on the motive that had forced the prisoner into killing. He pointed out the state of James Follett's mind when he committed the crime and especially dwelt on the part of Follett's statement where his wife had signified her intention of continuing to live in sin with his brother. In essence, said Winter, the accused did not know what he was doing and did not know right from wrong at the time.

Winter finished his long and able address about 1:30 P.M.

Wednesday Afternoon, June 17: In his summary of the trial, Crown prosecutor Kent refuted Winter's claim of an improper investigation. The prisoner did know what he was doing, but that much of his anxiety came from his wife's violent temper. When Constable Murphy came to the home, Follett did not make formal complaints of the alleged wrongs of Sis, but only spoke of minor matters. Two years ago the prisoner said he had come upon his brother and his wife in the act of committing adultery. If he had slain his brother then it would still have been a question as to whether he was justified in doing so or not. But in intervening two years, according to the evidence, he was visiting his brother's house and appeared friendly with him.

"The truth is," said Kent, "the prisoner was brooding over revenge. The law will consider an act done in a gust of passion, but not an act done after there has been time for the passion to cool. There was no provocation at or near the time this deed was committed."

Kent concluded, saying there was no evidence of insanity or provocation.

Judge Pinsent's charge to the jury was lengthy, but he left three issues to them: one, whether the prisoner, James Follett, was guilty of murder; two, whether he was guilty of manslaughter; or three, whether he was insane when the act was committed.

The jury filed out at 5:15 P.M. and returned at 8:00 P.M. with a verdict of manslaughter. Before the sentence was given, Winter rose to ask the court to consider some matters. James Follett, he said, had already undergone considerable misery, trouble and suffering. He had, as was presented during the trial, borne a good character for conduct and work. He was a good husband, father and neighbour, and up to the time of the offence, had led a blameless life. Winter asked Pinsent to take into consideration the condition of the man's family, his young children – two boys and two girls – who were now without support. They apparently had no care and affection from the mother, who had already threatened to leave home and had been unfaithful in her household duties. In July, James Follett was sentenced to seven years hard labour in the His Majesty's Penitentiary in St. John's.

Some years later, in 1899, a man believed to be Francis Canning of St. John's was to be hanged at the "pen." His hooded executioner was of average height. If his face could have been seen, it would have been dark in complexion with dark hair. He reached up to place the noose around the neck, then stepped back to await the warden's instructions. The executioner remained motionless until the war-

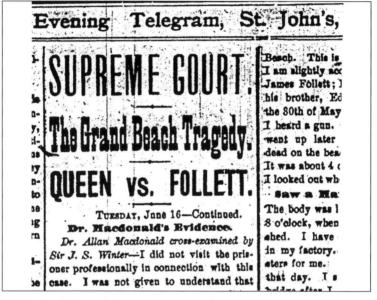

The *Evening Telegram* follows the murder trial. This section of the paper documents the testimony of Doctor Allan Macdonald, the physician who examined the body.

den nodded to him, then he pulled the lever sending the condemned man to his fate.

It is said from family sources the executioner was James Follett. In those days in Newfoundland a prisoner would be set free if he agreed to pull the lever in the final phase of a death penalty. This story doesn't quite ring true, considering Follett was due to be released in 1898, the year before Canning's execution. According to others, James Follett's work in prison was to make brooms, and he became proficient at the job and was a model prisoner. Upon release, James returned to Grand Beach where he lived out his days.

I'm Glad I Did It: Murder at Shore's Cove, Cape Broyle

It was a Saturday evening with civil weather and calm seas. John Yetman of St. Mary's figured he had to go ashore to get some items he needed for the next fishing voyage. The American schooner he worked on, *Helen F. Whitten*, stood off about 400 yards from Shore's Cove, a small fishing community near Cape Broyle harbour. Yetman climbed aboard the dory, untied the painter and was about to push off.

At the same time, three men from Cape Broyle, Ernest and Augustus Carew and J. Reddy, were coming into the harbour in their trap skiff and had just reached the wharf. They noticed the schooner and saw the young man climb into the dory. Then they heard three or four shots ring out, coming from the direction of the American banker. At the same time, the man in the dory near the schooner was seen to suddenly stand erect and then fall across the gunnel. The upper part of his body hung over the side and his head nearly touched the water.

The Carews and Reddy, sensing something terrible had happened, got back in their dory and rowed out to the schooner. They grabbed the slumping man who was still hanging over the gunnel to help him, but knew right away he was dead. They recognized the victim – John Yetman. He had been shot by the captain of *Helen F. Whitten*.

The Gloucester banker *Helen F. Whitten* had put into Cape Broyle on Newfoundland's east coast around the first of July 1903 for a supply of fresh bait and ice. The schooner had its problems ever since it left the United States in late March. Captain Frank Wollard had little fish, his crew didn't like his demeanor and many had jumped ship. Wollard, who was born and had lived in Central Argyle, near Yarmouth, Nova Scotia, was also a naturalized citizen of the United States. For his large American schooner which had often sailed short-handed, he recruited dorymen from the southern Avalon and Burin Peninsula.

Among his new crew was a hard-working young man from St. Mary's in St. Mary's Bay, John Yetman, destined to be the victim of a shooting tragedy. Yetman had already narrowly missed death during the voyage of the *Whitten*. While hauling trawls during a spate of thick fog, he and his dory mate, John Penny, went astray in their dory and spent four days and nights adrift. They were picked up by a French banker which transferred them to another vessel headed for the southern Avalon. That schooner dropped them off at Cape Broyle as Yetman and Penny knew the Whitten was going there for bait and ice.

However the vessel was not in Cape Broyle when the two castaways arrived, so they rowed to Bay Bulls (about 15 miles) to see if *Helen F. Whitten* was there. On July 1, the schooner did arrive in Cape Broyle and when Captain Wollard learned the missing men were at Bay Bulls, he telegraphed for them to return. Yetman and Penny then rowed back to Cape Broyle – Yetman little knowing he was going to his death.

Captain Wollard and his crew cheered when they arrived and the captain had been heard to say that Yetman was the best worker and fisherman aboard. Although he was delighted to see the two men back, Wollard's tune changed very quickly when, on Saturday, July 4, Yetman asked if he could go ashore.

Apparently John Yetman had enough of dory fishing, the possibility of going astray, and working under the iron rule of an American skipper. But he had signed on for a season, he couldn't or wouldn't just up and quit. Instead he asked if he could go ashore to pick up some personal items. There was plenty of time, he told the captain, before *Helen F. Whitten* sailed again for the banks.

But the captain pointed out that all the crew was aboard and busy getting the anchor up and the sails prepared. At that point Yetman became more adamant and said he was going anyway and untied the dory's painter or rope. Captain Wollard, in a fit of rage at losing another man and his best worker at that, pulled out his revolver. The captain thought Yetman would desert and leave the schooner shorthanded. That would be another delay.

Without speaking, he aimed the gun at Yetman. The first shot went through Yetman's heart, killing him instantly; then Wollard fired four other shots in rapid succession. Many crew became agitated or excited; others feared for their own lives. But Captain Wollard walked up and down the decks, making no attempt at hiding or trying to escape.

Meanwhile the Carews and Reddy had pulled up, made a quick examination of the body, and rowed back to shore to contact the local policeman. It had all happened so quickly, Yetman's shipmates – some of whom had known him for years – pulled him up from the dory to the deck. At first they hoped John Yetman had only been wounded and made an attempt to resuscitate him, but he was dead.

They fully expected Captain Wollard would make an attempt to escape by running the schooner out of the harbour, but he continued to pace the deck as if he had no idea of the terrible act he had just committed. After awhile he went to his cabin and locked the door.

A messenger alerted Cape Broyle's Constable Green and he came down to the wharf. In the King's Name, he asked for assistance; the two Carew's volunteered to go with him aboard the American vessel. The *Whitten's* crew said the captain had done the deed, but one of the crew, Joseph Walsh, had confiscated his revolver.

Green knocked on the cabin door and asked Wollard to surrender. In the captain's possession he found a 32-caliber revolver with four chambers containing empty shells. The captain then admitted he had shot Yetman and added he was glad he did it.

Constable Green put Wollard under arrest and asked him to come with him at once. By this time, word had spread around the harbour that a local man had been murdered. The crew of *Argo*, another banking vessel with a crew of several Newfoundland fishermen, were threatening to board *Helen F. Whitten*, beat down the cabin door, set fire to the schooner and inflict their own punishment on Wollard.

The constable did not handcuff the prisoner as they left *Helen F. Whitten* in a dory, fearing the boat might be attacked, and he wanted Wollard to have a chance to swim for his life. They landed at Carew's wharf and, thinking that other fishermen would come ashore and harm Wollard, Green immediately asked for a horse and cart to transport the accused murderer to Ferryland. It took two hours to get transportation and, during that time, one of Yetman's cousins came before Constable Green, swearing he would kill the captain. Green calmly talked to him and a second serious crime was averted.

Judge James Gerve Conroy arrived at Ferryland a few days later. Conroy stated Captain Wollard would have to be tried in St. John's for murder, but first he and Superintendent John J. Sullivan held a magisterial enquiry before committing the captain for trial.

The trial began on August 5, 1903. Captain Wollard's lawyers – Martin Williams Furlong and his assistant James Mary Kent – first asked to have case dismissed. They argued that Wollard was a citizen of the United States and the offence had been committed aboard an American vessel; thus may be out of Newfoundland's jurisdiction. Chief Justice Sir William Henry Horwood and Assistant Judges George Henry Emerson and George M. Johnson replied that since the crime had been committed in Cape Broyle harbour, it was clearly within their jurisdiction.

The first jury was dismissed, but on August 14, a second jury was selected: J.E. Furneaux, J. H. Jardine, N.J. Collier, Albert Wood, J. G. Hunt, R. Purcell, J.F. Canning, S.J. Feaver, W. K. Maddock, R. Cousins, W. Chancey and W.J. Ferd.

The first witnesses called was Joseph Walsh, a Placentia-born fisherman who resided in Boston. In his lengthy testimony he said he joined the vessel in March, stating that it was seven or eight crew short and had put into Fortune Bay for bait and crew. The *Whitten* afterwards sailed to Fox Cove, near Burin, to Cape St. Mary's and Placentia. After ten days fishing it put into Cape Broyle. Walsh described how Yetman and his dorymate Penny had gone astray and returned, how fishermen John Gosling had already jumped ship, and the anguish Wollard seemed to be in as Yetman asked to leave the schooner. He also described the events of July 4. The captain and many of the crew, he said, had been drinking at Carey's (or Carew) place, a well-known liquor and rum-smuggling establishment in Shore's Cove.

Constable Green testified he saw the five bullet holes in the body. When he went on board the schooner, he had vigorous resistance from Joseph Walsh and Thomas Hogan. With the assistance of the Carews, he overpowered Walsh and obtained Captain Wollard's revolver. Hogan said, in his testimony, he was too drunk on that day to remember anything.

Joseph Hartson of Burin, a crewman on *Helen F. Whitten*, stated that from where he stood on the quarter-deck he saw the captain draw the revolver and fire four shots at Yetman. He heard the captain say that if Yetman went ashore he would go dead.

Dr. Freebairn, the medical practitioner at Ferryland at the time, did the post-mortem on the body and gave evidence on the entrance and exit wounds. There followed on the stand several local residents who saw the body come ashore: Ernest Carew, Louis Williams and James Keefe of Cape Broyle. Edward Brien of St. John's said he was hired by Constable Green on the evening of July 4 to take the prisoner to Ferryland in his horse and cart. On the journey he said that Captain Wollard asked him if he had ever driven a murderer before. When Brien said no, Wollard replied, "Well, you're driving one now."

Several men took the stand for the defense as character witnesses for Captain Wollard. John Power of Tor's Cove made two voyages with Wollard in 1895 and 1896, finding him a competent master and good to his crew. James Byrne of Brigus South sailed with Wollard twelve years previously and saw no fault with the captain. M.P. Cashin, a politician (who later when on to become Prime Minister of Newfoundland), did business at Cape Broyle and had known the captain for 10 years. He recounted the troubles Wollard was having controlling his crew that summer. Cashin remarked to another person that he would not wish to be captain of an American vessel like that as all the members of the crew were captains, i.e. telling Wollard what to do.

Defense lawyer Furlong tried to establish that there was another fisherman aboard *Helen F. Whitten*, a troublesome giant of a man, who had threatened and beaten Wollard. Wollard carried a revolver to protect himself and no intention of murdering anyone. Defense also claimed that the captain was attempting to quell a mutiny when he shot and killed Yetman. After all Yetman was leaving ship against the captain's orders. This contention or theory was downplayed or undermined by prosecution.

The direct cause of the killing was that Yetman had said he was going ashore and the captain ordered him not to go, as the vessel was about to sail. Several crew gave evidence they had heard the captain say, "If he leaves the ship, he leaves it dead."

Ignoring the threat, Yetman jumped over the rail into the dory, and Wollard, who went to the rail with him,

Cape Broyle. One of the reasons why Newfoundland and American banking schooners went to Cape Broyle– a plentiful supply of fresh water.

pulled out his gun and fired four or five shots at the Newfoundland fishermen.

As the trial wound down and just before the jury was sent out to contemplate the verdict, the judges made a clear distinction between what constitutes manslaughter – an unplanned death perhaps resulting from sudden passion – and murder, planned or premeditated.

The verdict from the jury was "manslaughter." Wollard, age forty-eight and with a wife and three sons in Boston, was sentenced to sixteen years hard labour in the St. John's penitentiary.

Running the Blockade

A line of armed government ships manned with police blocked the entrance to Fortune Bay and St. Pierre – a sea barricade that prevented fishermen from Bay du Nord, Grand Bank, Fortune, Rencontre East, and other Fortune Bay towns from earning a living. The fishermen knew well that defiance of this sea wall would probably lead to arrest, then a trial and, if convicted, jail time in Harbour Breton. Or worse, in St. John's.

But it was desperate times and desperate times call for drastic actions and courageous people. Local vessels "ran the blockade," illegally squeezing through or skirting around the barrier. Normally, these vessels were manned law-abiding citizens – God-fearing men who, in this case, believed the law and the government were wrong to deprive them of the right to earn a livelihood.

The time of troubles began in 1888 when the government attempted, through a newly legislated Bait Act, to limit foreign over fishing in Newfoundland waters, a familiar story. The Bank fishery then was a hook and line fishery, and a good supply of fresh bait was essential. The provisions of the Bait Act prohibited Newfoundlanders from selling bait to foreign vessels and forbade them from coming in close to the coast where the necessary squid, herring and capelin were to be had. It had the support of most Newfoundland fishermen, except those in areas like Fortune Bay where good money could be made from the sale of bait to foreigners.

The bait was the highly-prized herring, a species which prior to the 1900s amassed in great schools in Fortune Bay. The large French fleet, dependant upon bait to fish, paid good prices and the local people appreciated the business. In 1883, for example, there were over three hundred Newfoundland craft supplying bait to the French; Grand Bank alone employed seven boats and thirty-five men.

Revenue Cutter "FIONA" of Nfld in the early 1900

The 164-ton revenue cutter *Fiona* (above) spent several weeks in Fortune Bay quelling an uprising over the "Bait Act." On May 23, 1925, it struck Trinity Ledge in the Bay of Fundy and sank. Captain Lew Blandford, mate Whelan and the 17 crew rowed into Port Maitland and went to Yarmouth, Nova Scotia.

"It was hazardous to sail on her," one of the crew said. "*Fiona* was over 40 years old and a wooden craft." In its lifetime the ship had been a private yacht, a revenue cutter for the Newfoundland government, and finally a workhorse in the coastal trade. At the time of its loss the steamer, then owned by Mr. Bennegar of St. John's, was headed to St. John's laden with bunker coal and 3000 sacks of potatoes.

By 1891, the French fishery, hampered by the lack of bait, offered Newfoundlanders five dollars per barrel of herring. It was a profitable trade that sparked several clashes with the law.

In April of that year, according to *The Newfoundland Quarterly*, Winter 2000 issue, "one hundred thirty craft of all sizes and descriptions descended upon Bay de East at the head of Fortune Bay" to catch herring and take it to St. Pierre. This, of course, was in an open defiance of the law.

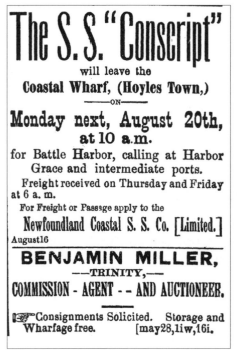

The S. S. "Conscript"

will leave the
Coastal Wharf, (Hoyles Town,)
————ON————

Monday next, August 20th, at 10 a.m.

for Battle Harbor, calling at Harbor Grace and intermediate ports.

Freight received on Thursday and Friday at 6 a. m.

For Freight or Passage apply to the

Newfoundland Coastal S. S. Co. [Limited.]
August16

BENJAMIN MILLER,
—TRINITY,—
COMMISSION - AGENT - - AND AUCTIONEER.

☞Consignments Solicited. Storage and Wharfage free. [may28,1iw,16i.

Ad for goods and services for *Conscript*, a vessel which participated in the Fortune Bay skirmish. This vessel, built in 1882, eventually changed its name to *Virginia Lake*. On April 8, 1909, while engaged in the seal fishery, it was damaged in an ice floe and partially sank. The crew set the vessel on fire to prevent it from becoming a navigational hazard.

As a counter measure, the government sent the revenue cutters SS *Fiona* and SS *Lady Glover* from St. John's to enforce the Bait Act. *Fiona* was commanded by James Fanning McGrath, born on Oderin Island, Placentia Bay but a resident of St. John's. McGrath had been appointed

Commissioner for the Bait Protection Service in the Whiteway government.

One April day a small boat manned by a lone police officer overtook a craft bound to St. Pierre from Bay du Nord and commanded by a man named Banfield, whose first name has not been recorded. The lawman ordered Banfield to heave to, which he ignored. The *Fiona* steamed closer and the crew launched the ship's boat and rowed alongside. When the police officer jumped on deck of the Bay du Nord vessel, Banfield and two other men lifted him up in their arms and tossed him into the sea as coolly as if he were a bag of hay.

He was rescued none the worst for his ducking. *Fiona* took possession of the craft and towed it into Harbour Breton where the law-defying individuals were handed over to authorities.

One policeman, Eli Miles of St. John's, described his role in the blockade saying (in the magazine *Atlantic Guardian*, January 1949) that he was on the SS *Fiona* when it was sent out from St. John's to enforce the Bait Act. He and 30 other police, headed by Sub-Inspector Sullivan, manned the steamer. They wore the "bobby" uniforms similar to the outfits worn by police in England.

By April 20, the SS *Hercules* with ten constables aboard arrived at Bay de East and rumours circulated that the government had ordered a gunboat from Halifax to proceed to Fortune Bay. Nine days later the SS *Conscript* left St. John's with a detachment of 15 regular constables and twenty special (civilian) police.

By this time the outlaw fishing fleet – the numbers ranging from 35 to 40 vessels, depending on which historical account one reads – headed to St. Pierre. Most had its name painted over or covered with canvas to prevent easy identification. Four steamers each with a contingent of police, strategically placed at the entrance to the bay, off St. Pierre, had no chance to stopping the remaining insurrectionists. A local historian, Aaron Buffett of Grand Bank, described the events as viewed from Grand Bank:

> A flotilla of herring skippers conspired to defy authority. Forty vessels sailed together, approached the waters off Green Island and St. Pierre, and passed by with the revenue cutters cruising among them. Women, children and non-fishermen stood on the headlands at Grand Bank and Fortune watching the skirmish in Fortune Bay.

On April 29, the blockade-running vessels, having eluded the law and successfully landed their cargo at St. Pierre, tri-

Prisoners on the CONSCRIPT, 1891	
John Pittman	Rencontre East
M. Roper	Rencontre East
William Hartigan	Rencontre East
George Pope	Stone's Cove
John Vallis	Coomb's Cove
Jerry Petite (Jr.)	Mose Ambrose
Thomas Hynes	Bay L'Argent
D. McCarthy	Head of Bay (later renamed Terrenceville)

umphantly sailed into St. Jacques. *The Evening Herald* reported (May 2, 1891) "*Fiona, Lady Glover,* and *Favourite* followed helplessly. The men on the schooners threatened to fire at them if they were interfered with."

Once in St. Jacques harbour, calmer heads prevailed. Denis Burke, who owned Burke's extensive fish procuring premises there, persuaded those with outstanding warrants for arrest to give themselves up. Several men were arrested; most were released from lack of evidence and in the end only eight prisoners sailed to St. John's on the *Conscript.*

Despite the vast flotilla of blockade runners, only one vessel was actually seized and taken under armed escort – probably to Harbour Breton. On April 30, while under surveillance from *Fiona* and *Favourite*, two schooners known to have broken the law left Bay de East. *Fiona* followed one, a vessel operated by a Mr. Kirby who dealt at Burke's business at St. Jacques. Kirby's schooner had carried 300 barrels of herring to St. Pierre – 200 barrels sold at three dollars a barrel and the rest at one dollar per barrel. Apparently Kirby and his crew then slipped away to the fishing banks and didn't return to Fortune Bay, at least not for the law to see.

Favourite chased the second vessel with more success. Its crew captured a schooner, skippered by T. Grandy and owned by Enrico Giovannani, a businessman of St. Jacques. This ship was known to have delivered 180 barrels of herring to the French. Grandy was held in custody on board *Fiona* which had the facilities for prisoners. *Fiona* also arrested another fleet ringleader who had put into Belleoram.

The eight men brought to St. John's aboard *Conscript* were arraigned before a magistrate on May 2, 1891, then escorted to the penitentiary until their trial date, May 16 with Judge Prowse presiding.

Trial day came quickly and ended even more so. Lawyer Thomas J. Murphy spoke for the crown and called only one witness, Constable Sheppard. Sheppard testified he saw the bait aboard a Fortune Bay craft as it headed to St. Pierre. The defence, led by Sir J.S. Winter (James Spearman who later became Prime Minister of Newfoundland.) argued the fishermen did not have to stop or "heave to" under orders from *Fiona* as they were not on the high seas. Winter knew the Bait Act definition of "high seas" was not clear nor specific.

Seven were found not guilty and released. Thomas Hynes and William Steward (who was not present at the trial) were found guilty and released on bail of five hundred dollars. Newspaper reporters and the general populace of St. John's were amused by the ineptitude and bungling of the police. The law was ineffective; the police a laughing stock and Bait Act flotilla was a farce. Publications of the day like *Evening Herald* (May 2, 1891) pounced on the fact that the cruisers were powerless to prevent a recurrence of the "Bait Act" troubles and sympathized with the fishermen. "This breach of the law," the paper claimed, "is much to be regretted and that [the people of Fortune Bay] will calmly wait the fulfilment of the promise of compensation made to them by the Newfoundland Government."

Throughout the summer of 1891, letters and arguments flew back and forth from Fortune Bay to St. John's newspapers. South Coast fishermen sent scathing letters and stated their unfortunate situation in the local papers. The May 4, 1891, edition of *The Evening Telegram* had a letter entitled "Running the Blockade" from Belleoram to Long Harbour, Fortune Bay which claimed:

> ...large quantities of herring are going to St. Pierre in Newfoundland and American banking schooners. One banker, from Burin, arrived at St. Pierre with 250 barrels of herring on board. Why should the Government refuse our Fortune Bay men so severely for taking one trip of herring, to keep off starvation?
> We plead for justice.
>
> (signed) Fortune Bay

By the time the dust of the Fortune Bay affray settled, several local fishermen spent time in the Harbour Breton jail, in the St. John's penitentiary, or in irons aboard *Fiona*. Those that eluded the cutters were chased and manhunts ensued as daring lawbreakers tried to outwit law officers. In the end though law and order prevailed, as it usually does.

Education and prevention are often effective measures to deter crime and illegal activities. In the months after the Fortune Bay insurrection, fishermen were asked to refrain from selling their bait to the French. In St. John's and larger outports, posters were circulated pointing out the long-term effects of selling bait. One such poster read:

Of course, none of these squabbles and shennagians between the English fishermen and the Newfoundland

> NEWFOUNDLANDERS, BE MEN!
> STARVE IF YOU MUST:
> BUT HANG ON TO YOUR HERRING!
>
> P.S. If you sell your bait to the French now you are bound to starve in the long run.

police perturbed the French. They were still able to get some bait illegally from Newfoundland fishermen (some of the fishermen claimed the herring was intended for food for St. Pierre kitchen tables) and the French fished as they always did.

As a footnote of human interest, there remains other related anecdotes to the Bait Act dust-up. Some years ago I spoke to an elderly gentleman, George Foote, whose family operated a cod procuring and exporting business in Grand Bank in the heyday of the Bait Act. Sometime prior to 1900, his ancestor, Morgan Foote, owned a vessel engaged in the bait smuggling business. The name, *Smuggler*, perhaps helps verify this. According to Foote's recollection it was indeed used to smuggle bait to the French.

To avoid detection in the time of the bait act troubles, *Smuggler's* nameplate had been removed; in effect the little schooner carried no name nor place of registry to identify it. At a stopover in St. Pierre, the French police, or gendearms, were curious and asked, "What's the name of this schooner?"

"None of your damned business!" the captain replied. The gendearms hurried off in a huff intending to get other police to arrest the insolent captain or to impound the vessel. By the time reinforcements arrived, the name "None of Your Damn Business" was painted on the bow. Peace was restored, tempers cooled off, and both parties continued business as usual.

According to family history, George Pope's vessel in the 'Fortune Bay Skirmish' was the *William Henry Jane*. This ship, named for George's three children, was a jackboat with its rudder fitted outside on the stern.

In the fall of 1901 or 1902, James Elms and his son, Albert, borrowed the *William Henry Jane* and went to Great Jarvois to cut timber for a house. With the two men aboard, the boat broke its mooring in the night, drifted out of Fortune Bay – the boat and two crew were never seen again.

Both men belonged to Stone's Cove. Albert, aged twenty-six, was married to Rosie Riggs and his father James, fifty-two, was survived by his wife Charlotte (Pope).

Send Extra Police – Immediately

In John Crosbie's article 'The Boom in Municipal Government' (a section in Smallwood's *The Book of Newfoundland* Volume IV) one finds this sentence: "In 1943 Grand Bank's town council was incorporated by a Special Act." As it turned out the memories of how the council came in was special for many people of the day. It was action all right, and the reaction was an explosion of unnecessary ill-feeling and deeds of violence.

Civil unrest; all work at a standstill; the general populace, in a foul and ugly mood, gather on the town bridge shouting threats; reports of light poles being sawn down or planned arson of government buildings; jail sentences and fines; over 50 policemen take back the town bridge and parade through the narrow streets in a show of power. This scene doesn't ring true for a small Newfoundland town of fifty years ago; but it was the situation in Grand Bank in the summer of 1944.

In his book *The Newfoundland Constabulary*, author Arthur Fox also makes reference to a disturbance at Grand Bank in July 1944. According to Fox, on the fourteenth of July the general population openly expressed their opposition to the newly-formed town council. On that day three Grand Bank business firms and two drivers were convicted in court for breaches of council regulations. Many people became indignant, defied authorities and interfered with the efforts of local police, the Rangers, doing their duty.

These brief descriptions in obscure books belie or understate the actual fireworks and state of turmoil that transpired in Grand Bank. The clash, the fireworks, now known locally as "the riot on the bridge" can best come from those at the scene – the rioters and the police who tried to uphold the law.

Public discontent began on December 28 of the previous year when Newfoundland's Commission of Government (Division of Public Health and Welfare), supported by a petition from Magistrate Herman Quinton and several townspeople, approved a request to incorporate Grand Bank thus giving the town council legal status.

Many Grand Bankers, for fear of increased taxation, were opposed to the new council. Those who met on street corners and at work not only grumbled and cursed, but openly planned forums of public protest. Some months later a counter-petition signed by one hundred and eleven citizens was sent to Quinton who rejected their petition outright. "Too many are signed with no name and merely marked with an X," he said. These people, Quinton claimed, were illiterate, unable to write and thus did not understand what they were signing.

At this point, the spring of 1944, perhaps a better selling job or a public education campaign would have changed the views of opponents, but it was not to be. Commission of Government had decided to use Grand Bank, a self-sufficient and industrious town, as a test case for a fishing community. Local government came in, literally and figuratively, with a shove and a push.

Grand Bank Working People Out On Strike

No Release On Situation From Government As Yet—Several Convicted Now Gaoled

THE action of the Government in sending a squad of policemen to
~ ' Bank has resulted in rather sensational developments in

The *Daily News* puts the events of July 20-21, 1944, on its front page, saying the government sent a "squad of police" to Grand Bank to quell a riot.

In June, Sir John Puddister, Commissioner of Public Health and Welfare, came to the divided Grand Bank to incorporate it as a municipality. As the June tenth edition of *The Evening Telegram* reported, "The antis are still active and the Commissioner's visit, it is understood, is for the purpose of allaying the fears of those who oppose the measure because of the taxation involved."

Fears of the working class townspeople were not put to rest. Several citizens who refused to pay town taxes were cheered by supporters as they paid small fines and left the courthouse. To crush this blatant show of resistance and to assist the two Rangers stationed at Grand Bank (Nathan Penney and another policeman), Sergeant Ian Glendinning, who was also in Grand Bank assessing the situation, requested that a squad of fifty Newfoundland Constabulary be sent from St. John's to restore peace. By July nineteenth, the fifty Constabulary, lead by District Inspector William Case, had arrived along with Ranger reinforcements from St. Lawrence and Lamaline.

Years before, Case had lived in Grand Bank as a young police officer; some of his children were born in Grand Bank. Knowing the quiet, law-abiding people, Case couldn't understand why they were rioting and was determined to find out who or what was causing the problem.

Feelings still ran deep among those who felt local government would impose restrictions and levy unnecessary taxes. Many opponents of the council had already refused to pay taxes and, to show their resentment of the arrival of the police, a general strike was called for July twentieth.

In essence, the labourers or general workers were in complete control of the town's economy. Women cured the fish on the beaches, men brought the salt bulk fish to them, carried the dried product to the fish stores where inside workers culled, pressed and packaged the finished product into barrels for overseas markets. Hundreds of quintals of fish representing thousands of dollars and weeks of toil on the fishing grounds were left unattended on the beaches. In those days there were no unions, but the power of the people could not be underestimated. Each worker convinced others that if work stopped, the town and the emerging council would be on the brink of economic collapse.

A group of three well-known businessmen were self-appointed leaders of the opposition – brothers Don and Fred Tibbo, taximen, and druggist Howard Patten. In a gentlemen's agreement, all three planned to resist authority and to refuse to pay any taxes. Both Tibbos were convicted and served a short time in the Burin holding cell. When Don and Fred Tibbo found out Patten had recanted, both immediately paid any fines and were released.

Patten, a vocal dissenter and community leader, had considerable holdings and property; thus would be taxed heavily. He promised to deliver an anti-council speech on the Grand Bank bridge around seven o'clock that evening.

Fred Hancock, a young policeman stationed in St. John's, was one of the fifty who arrived on the SS *Home*. Now retired from the Constabulary and living in St. John's, he vividly remembers those unsettled days in Grand Bank.

> We left St. John's by train, arrived in Argentia and travelled to Grand Bank by steamer. I remember we went in the harbour in the evening and I thought the town was a compact place – the houses were near together and the streets so narrow. Ken Moore and I stayed at Buffett's – Aaron Buffett's house. Others were all scattered around; some in the Harris' homes and some at the Thorndyke Hotel. Case stayed in the Ranger's home (once located near present-day Warren's Store).

By the evening of the nineteenth, news filtered down to Inspector Case that more trouble was brewing. Case decided to wait it out for twenty-four hours; perhaps by overnight cooler heads would prevail. But the next day practically all work in the fish stores and on the fish curing beaches ceased. Workers, men and women, milled around

The Ranger's Quarters in Grand Bank in 1935. The "God Save the King" sign and British flags help celebrate King George V's Silver Jubilee. The section extending (left) behind was the jail. Also (left) is the roof of Morgan Penwell's house. The people (right) are ready for a parade or public function.
    Police Inspector William Case stayed here during the council troubles in 1944. Case knew the people of the town well for he was stationed in Grand Bank in 1927-28 as a young Sergeant. At least one of his children was born there.

the waterfront and main streets discussing and damming the state of affairs "higher-ups" in St. John's and Grand Bank had gotten them into. After supper nearly everyone in town was along Water Street or on Grand Bank bridge hoping to hear Patten's analysis of the burdens of taxation and the drawbacks of local government.

Meanwhile all that day, Case knew what was about to happen. He assembled his detachment in front of the Sons of Temperance Hall, near the town's main street. Hancock was there and remembered special instructions

Inspector Case said, 'Now I want everybody in full uniform by the courthouse at six o'clock.' He gave us a speech outside the courthouse on how to manage a mob scene. At seven o'clock that night the people were going to have this meeting on the bridge. We had to turn up with our batons and handcuffs and everything like that. The only ammunition we had was tear gas which, as it turned out, we didn't have to use.

We marched in pairs up to the bridge and there Case stood on the rail and addressed the crowd. He made a wonderful job of it – he could handle a situation like that – and reproached the people.

Case, realizing World War II was still being fought, used patriotism as part of his speech. I don't remember all his words, but in essence he said to the hundreds of people gathered,

> You're helping the enemy by refusing to make fish. The fish is needed; the food is needed to feed our people, our soldiers and sailors overseas. Go back to your homes or your place of businesses. The law of your town's incorporation is passed which says you have to pay your taxes. If you don't you will be punished.
>
> I will give you ten minutes to leave the area for this is an unlawful assembly. You can't assemble in large numbers without the written consent of the magistrate. It becomes an unlawful assembly so I require of you to go back to your homes. You have ten minutes and if you don't move willingly, you'll be moved forcibly. Anyone who refuses to go will be arrested.

Case, Glendinning, Penney, Hancock, Moore, Norman Crane, William Costigan, Carter, Lethbridge, Legrow and some fifty other police lined up shoulder to shoulder along the street on both sides leading up to the bridge, securing the roadway and any access to the bridge. When Case's ten minutes expired, he gave the order to move the crowd and clear the streets. Hancock recalled the rush:

> Well, people went in all directions. As we pushed along the road, they'd fill up a front yard there, and fill up a lane or an alleyway somewhere else. Anyway we cleared the roads and we kept marching back and forth. By and by darkness set in. We kept on parading back and forth there until nightfall and people gradually went to their homes.

Businessman Patten, who had refused to pay his taxes and who had planned to lecture on the bridge, was arrested and brought before Magistrate Beaton Abbott the next day. Constable Hancock was there, as were all police gathered in or around the Temperance Hall which had been converted into a temporary courthouse. They would prevent any large crowds from gathering and obstructing justice.

While he stood guard outside the courthouse, Hancock recalled an elderly lady (Maggie Stone), incensed over the arrests and frustrations of those against the council, grabbed up a large rock and threatened to strike one of the policemen. She too was arrested and came before court that day. Mrs. Stone refused to answer any questions fired at her by Abbott and would only reply, "I'm not going to say."

She only changed her answer once when Abbott asked the final question: Mrs. Stone, do you plea guilty or not guilty? To this she replied, "I knows, but I'm not going to say!"

After a stern lecture Magistrate Abbott fined Mrs. Stone $25.00. "I don't care what it is," she fumed. "I'm not paying a cent!"

When Patten's case came up, as Hancock remembered it, he was fined $70.00 and the magistrate explained to him that

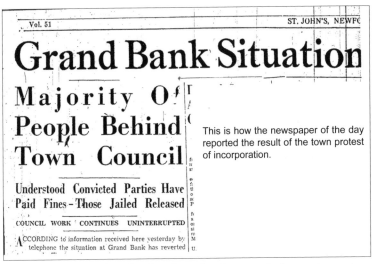

Vol. 51   ST. JOHN'S, NEWF(

Grand Bank Situation

Majority Of
People Behind
Town Council

This is how the newspaper of the day reported the result of the town protest of incorporation.

Understood Convicted Parties Have Paid Fines – Those Jailed Released

COUNCIL WORK CONTINUES UNINTERRUPTED

ACCORDING to information received here yesterday by telephone the situation at Grand Bank has reverted

this was a fine for disobeying the law and for not paying town taxes. Abbott meant business. He fined Patten, but gave him an alternative – time in jail. Sometime that day, when Patten learned the prison term would be served in St. John's, he recanted, apologized and paid the fine as well as his taxes. He also talked to Mrs. Stone, paid her fine and she was released.

Patten's change of heart and reversal of fortunes was also related to a simple matter of business and the bottom line of a ledger sheet. He was the only druggist in the area served by the Grand Bank Cottage Hospital, an area encompassing the towns from Lamaline to Garnish; thus, his services (and his potential loss of income) were significant.

For two days during the protest the fish had been left unattended on the beaches and during this time the weather remained sunny and clear. If it had rained, thousands of quintals of fish would have spoiled and the economic losses to several businesses would have been disastrous.

Within a week the tension subsided; work resumed and tardy taxpayers visited the newly-formed council. Most of the constabulary returned to St. John's, but about twenty remained for an extra week or so. Each day around noon they had to go out on patrol until dark. Hancock was one who stayed on after the situation returned to normal.

> On a Saturday the Buffett family invited us to go down to their summer home at Famine, outside of Grand Bank. Moore and I thought it over. Everything fell quiet: court cases were over, Patten paid his fine and turned over. As I recall Famine was a beautiful place. We also went to Lamaline, down to Piercey's Brook trouting right out near the salt water.

In 1927 the bridge (above) was constructed. In 1983-84 this was demolished for a more modern structure – the Frederick M. Tessier Bridge. The bridge became the focal point for a clash between those who wanted local government and its opponents. Inspector Case stood on the concrete railing (left) to address the hundreds of dissatisfied townspeople.

Now while we were in Grand Bank an old gentleman, I think his name was Foote, a retired captain, passed away (July 21). None of us saw him because he was in bed, but he died while we were there. We went to his funeral with all hands marching in procession.

One morning after we were all back in St. John's, we assembled in the drill hall in Fort Townsend. The inspector read us a letter from the townspeople of Grand Bank. It was in appreciation for our services.

The attendance at the burial services of Thomas Foote and also Sarah Forsey (d. July 23, 1944), became a goodwill public gesture which helped reconcile the town towards the intrusion of police, plus the realization of council benefits which convinced the striking workers to go back to

The business of the fish trade, Grand Bank 1927-28. Man centre is William Forsey of fish procuring-trading business, man left is Harvey Thomas, the engineer who designed and helped build Grand Bank Bridge. The women left are those who work on the fish drying beaches with traditional long white sun bonnet and white skirts. Foreground are salt fish laid on beach for drying, a pile or "pook" of fish, the culling or grading table, (right) and a cart to take the graded fish to the fish store. Photo faces north with Grand Bank in the background.

work. When outstanding taxes were paid and the newly-appointed council members transacted the town's business, the public expression of dissatisfaction quietly ended.

The first council meeting was held in the Newfoundland Rangers' headquarters, a building which once stood near present-day Warren's Store. The headquarters measured thirty-six feet long and contained three prisoners' cells – suitable for short confinement i.e. those arrested during the council riot. Later the building was purchased by Onslow Brown who sold it to businessman Harold Warren. It was taken down in 1947.

Ironically, a few years after the council riot Howard Patten, to complete a turnaround in belief, ran in a Grand Bank municipal election and won a seat, lending credence to the old maxim, "If you can't beat 'em, join 'em." After he retired from the constabulary, William Case was superintendent in the Newfoundland Penitentiary and he also helped establish the Salmonier Prison Farm, a novel concept in Canada's prison system.

Fifty years ago. Fifty policemen. A summer of discontent when Grand Bank became the third municipality in Newfoundland after Windsor and Corner Brook East to become incorporated and to enjoy the benefits of local government.

The Warship Cornwall and the Siege of Flat Island

HMS *Cornwall*, a 9,800-ton British cruiser, left St. John's for Bonavista Bay on Monday, June 30, 1919. The great armoured ship, which had seen action at the Falkland Islands during World War I, was heading for Flat Island, Bonavista Bay. It was a daunting foray into the bay for British naval officers, many of whom had never been to Newfoundland before. They had charts of the coast, but fog, hidden reefs, even icebergs could make short work of His Majesty's Ship. To ensure a safe voyage *Cornwall's* commander, Captain H.K. Kitson R.N., took on local pilot Captain William Carrol. The British Admiralty certainly took a risk sending one of the top ships of its fleet to a rather obscure island in Bonavista Bay, but why?

Part of the answer lies in an editorial in *The Evening Telegram* (July 7, 1919) by the paper's reporter at the time, Joseph R. Smallwood. Smallwood went on the trip to Flat Island and his story, The Cruise of HMS *Cornwall*, begins with: "*Cornwall* set a course to the scene of the trouble brought about by the refusal of the people of Flat Island to permit the police to search their houses for illicit intoxicants which, they had good reasons for believing, had been brewed by the islanders and was being distributed by them." In essence, the Flat Islanders were brewing and selling moonshine.

To the young reporter Smallwood and the citizens of St. John's who flocked to the waterfront to view this mighty ship, the majesty of the British navy was evident. *Cornwall* had twin engines of 22,000 horsepower; it carried 32 officers, 52 cadets with the remainder of the crew sailors and marines. The ship even sported a military band which played while the crew took their twice daily jog around the deck.

HMS *Cornwall* had seen plenty of action during the Great War; that was physically evident in its center funnel, riddled with shrapnel holes. It had fought a great battle at the Falkland Islands on December 8, 1914, when it sank the German ship *Leipzic*. During the exchange of fire a piece of shell entered *Cornwall's* galley and killed two men. It was also one of the ships that trapped the enemy cruiser *Koenigsberg* at the mouth of the Rufiji River in East Africa.

On the first night of the voyage to Bonavista Bay, the *Cornwall* anchored off New Perlican. At 7:00 A.M. the next morning it stopped off Grate's Point where there was a large iceberg, about 300 foot long and 50 foot high. The ship carried 8 six-inch guns on deck, but these had not been fired in six months. Off Grate's Point, Newfoundland, the crew got in a few practice rounds at the berg. "When the guns sounded," Smallwood said, "the firing was certainly the loudest sound ever heard by me."

From four miles away *Cornwall* let loose the cannons: the after turret guns, followed by the after casement gun; the ship turned around so that the port guns fore and aft were discharged – 72 rounds in total. Everyone aboard had their ears stuffed with cotton and the vibrations nearly demolished one of the officer's cabins. Not much of the berg remained when firing ceased.

All this fire power, show and military pageantry was not lost on the real purpose of the *Cornwall*'s cruise – to apprehend a few Flat Island fishermen. In May 1919 police in St. John's received reliable reports that some people on Flat Island were distilling homebrew, or moonshine, and passing it around or selling it. Authorities sent Constable John Summers to investigate and at Greenspond he was joined by another constable. On Coward's Island, near Flat Island, they searched four houses but found nothing. Off Flat Island, they were met by three motor boats containing about 50 men. Summers identified himself and began asking questions about the illegal brews.

In no uncertain terms the Flat Island men told Summers to leave. Back in Greenspond Summers telegraphed Police Inspector General Charles Henry Hutchings in St. John's. Inspector General Hutchings sent eight police by train to Gambo and thence to Greenspond to assist Summers in completing his investigation. These were Sergeant Savage, Head Constable Noseworthy, Constables Peddle, Kelly, Wade, Simmonds, Way and Lee. Sergeant Forsey, who at the time, was stationed at Gambo joined them, as well as Constable Tucker who was stationed at Greenspond.

Summers and his contingent, along with Greenspond's Magistrate Isaac James Mifflin, arrived on Flat Island, hoping to arrest the leaders and to get to the bottom of the illegal distillation. But when word came that the police had returned, Flat Islanders turned out in numbers – some sources say about fifty men armed with muzzle loaders and 'swiling' guns. They hid behind rocks, stages and fences, warning the police to leave.

There is probably as much disagreement over who had arms and who threatened whom as there were people at the scene. Stories of an armed stand-off vary. Opponents of the government saw the police as instigators. William F. Coaker, President of the Fishermen's Protective Union, writing in the *Fishermen's Advocate* said:

> I learn from a man from Flat Island that the first police to visit searched four houses and found no liquor. Subsequently ten armed police with Mifflen came to arrest some men. They landed at Samson's wharf; nine men (of Flat Island) walked down to the wharf and did not even have a pocket knife. Immediately nine rifles were pointed at the men on the wharf. The men on the wharf saw some police putting cartridges into rifles.
>
> This is what caused the resentment and excitement: the want of discretion in the beginning and turning trivial matters into mountains.

At any rate Summers again retreated. At Greenspond he sent another telegram to the police inspector, appealing for help or reinforcements.

At that time, late June1919, HMS *Cornwall* was visiting St. John's. When word of further trouble reached the city, Newfoundland's Attorney General, Alfred B. Morine, contacted the British Admiralty to have the *Cornwall* steam to Flat Islands. By Tuesday evening July 1, it had picked up Magistrate Mifflin and the team of police at Greenspond, proceeded to Salvage Bay – about six miles southwest from Flat Island – to anchor. On Friday morning the large steam pinnace and a cutter were launched from *Cornwall* and the invasion of Flat Island began.

By early July there were few able-bodied men left on Flat Island. In the intervening days between the visit of the police and the arrival of the armed cruiser, most men had gone away to the Labrador fishery. Smallwood, the reporter on the scene, wrote:

> The Marines numbered forty-eight, and the reminder of the party which numbered ninety all told, were served out revolvers, ammunition...and a Maxim machine gun, capable of firing six hundred shots a minute, was set in the bow of the cutter. At 8:00 A.M. a start was made on our three mile trip to Flat Island.
>
> ...When the boats came up to and berthed alongside the public wharf nobody was to be seen and the reception that had been expected was missing. A few women and children could be seen farther back, while on the wharf itself was a woman with a child in her arms.
>
> This did not deceive the landing party, however, as it was felt it might easily have been a trap and that behind the boulders lay hidden dozens of desperate men, armed with sealing guns, ready to

die, if necessary, before allowing the police to arrest them.

If all were given arms, then the reporter, as part of the siege, had a revolver too. But the few remaining men on Flat Island offered no resistance to anyone. The invading force arrested seven men they suspected were ringleaders

HMS *Cornwall* (1902-1920), the fourth British warship bearing that name, was a 9,000 ton armoured cruiser launched at Pembroke, England, in 1902. It visited Newfoundland and sailed the rocky waters on Bonavista Bay in 1919. The next year it was de-commissioned and scrapped.

of the group that had resisted police a few days before. In the skirmish the police forgot one important aspect (or maybe it was overlooked intentionally to keep the peace). No one collected any evidence of moonshining – there was no raid to find the illegal stills, no equipment was brought back as evidence, and no statements were taken of who was doing what.

On July 5, HMS *Cornwall* arrived back in St. John's with the seven alleged suspects: Arthur Samson, Nathan and Job Chaytor, Fred Kelligrews, Wilfred Decker, John Morgan and Israel Ralph. They were charged on two counts, obstructing police in the discharge of their duty and, with loose and disorderly conduct. All pleaded "not guilty." The Department of Justice wanted this embarrassing fiasco to be over with as soon as possible. Besides the Flat Island men were away from their life work which they could ill afford to miss.

In the meantime the St. John's harbour tug *D.P. Ingraham*, commanded by Captain Marmaduke Rose, had been sent to the Labrador to find and arrest more men of Flat Island implicated in the disturbances. Six police went along: Sergeant O'Neill, Sergeant Forsey, Constables Simmonds, Lee, Kelly and Peddle. The men they were looking for were all on various fishing vessels in the Strait of Belle Isle and were arrested without trouble. The tug went as far as Francis Harbour for two others, but they could not be found. On July 24, *D.P.*

ꓤUNDLAND, JULY 8, 1919—4

The "Flat Island" Trial
Crown Withdraws Charge of 'Rioting' and Substitutes Other Charges
ANOTHER POSTPONEMENT THIS MORNING.

The papers of the day, July 8, 1919, say the crown had withdrawn the charge of 'rioting' against Flat Island men brought to St. John's for trial.

Ingraham brought back Aaron Ralph, John Hallett, Lewis Ralph, Reuben Ralph, Edward Morgan and Thomas Butt.

Magistrate Alfred Penney, brought in from Carbonear, presided over the trial. However, in court there was much confusion coupled with government interference and innuendo. Charges of rioting were dropped and other charges were substituted. Police had not gathered needed evidence for the brewing of illegal liquor and no charges were brought forward for that offence. No one knew if the men in custody were the ones who had actually confronted police on Flat Island.

All defendants were discharged. They returned home to resume their legal fishing occupations or to pursue any other illegal activities. Before *Cornwall* departed St. John's for England, Captain William Carrol, who had taken the

Flat Island, Bonavista Bay. Moored there is the 112-ton schooner *Effie May Petite*. It was built at Shelburne, Nova Scotia, in 1913 for Jeremiah Petite of English Harbour West and was eventually sold to Captain Job Kean of Brookfield, Bonavista Bay. Kean sold the schooner to Jesse Howell of Pound Cove, but ended its days on the South Coast, beached and left to rot near Burin.

cruiser safely to Bonavista Bay and back, was honoured by the cruiser's captain and his name was entered on the list of Admiralty Pilots.

The people of Flat Island never forgot the infamous "Moonshine Rebellion" of 1919. As for the nineteen-year-old reporter, Joey Smallwood, he glorified the "Cruise of the *Cornwall*" excursion in his newspaper article. However, the anti-government newspaper *Evening Advocate,* in a letter dated July 8, claimed Smallwood had gone to Flat Island "armed to the teeth with an automatic revolver" as an aide-de-camp or private secretary for Inspector General Hutchings.

It must have been pathetic when a Flat Island woman dropped to her knees as her husband was taken away. She begged the Inspector General and his aide-de-camp reporter not to shoot him. Neither Hutchings nor Smallwood had the decency to tell the women, children or prisoners that no harm would come to them.

City reporters, the letter claimed, have a modest and peaceful life as pencil-pushers, but in their midst there was a modern Napoleon, a Marshal Foch or a General Haig. It concluded, "Steps should be taken to present the achievements of this heroic lad to the Governor and that a suitable medal be presented to him for his brave and fearless conduct at the Siege of Flat Island."

In his unpublished autobiography, Smallwood says, "I was accepted on board the *Cornwall* as the Inspector General's private secretary...We steamed around Bonavista Bay, gathered up a dozen policemen and fired broadside after broadside at icebergs until the very bay reverberated with the *Cornwall*'s gunfire and the voters of the Bay were well-cowed."

Disasters and Oddities

Wall of Water

About 10:00 P.M. Robert Hillier of Point au Gaul began to think of the dead and injured. Clarity of thought and action came to him only after the initial shock and horror of tidal wave, so foreign and remote in his isolated corner of the world, was momentarily put away in the recesses of his mind. While he and his own family survived, others were not so lucky.

Point au Gaul is one of those sheltered coves that ring the iron bound cliffs on the eastern side of Newfoundland's Burin Peninsula. First frequented over three hundred years ago by the French, the town's proximity to the wealth of the cod fishing grounds provided security and home to its small population of inshore fishermen. And today with its two hundred residents of English/Irish descent, Point au Gaul typifies most Newfoundland towns drawing its sustenance from nature's ocean bounty.

But the sea with its richness also has a power – beautiful, awesome, sometimes deadly, and when the violent forces of sea and earth collide the result can be devastating. On November 18, 1929, many people in Point au Gaul, Port au Bras, Burin, Taylor's Bay and Lord's Cove watched the sea unleash a terrible and destructive power. A wave estimated by some to be over sixty feet high, destroyed homes, sheds, stages and swept twenty-seven people along the coast to their death.

On that night about 7:00 P.M., Robert Hillier played cards, Auction Forty-Fives, at a friend's house, but somehow the usual laughter and banter were strangely subdued. Quiet conversation centred around an unexplained earth tremor which shook their houses, rattled windows and dishes two hours earlier. No one could explain it – an explosion somewhere, a cave in, a plane crash? Hillier remembers the moonlit night to be so still and tranquil it seemed to be a portend of disaster.

> After a while we heard the sea gurgling out of the cove and scrambled outside to see what was going on. The night was clear and we saw, oddly enough, there was no water left in the harbour. Someone shouted, 'Look at the wall of water coming!' Then a huge white boil of foam roared in.

Today when most people think of a tidal wave they recall the movie *Poseidon Adventure* – how survivors fought their way out of a luxury liner overturned by a wall of water. A tidal wave or tsunami is a group of waves triggered by an underground earthquake or mudslide. As the earth lifts or collapses it moves tons of water above it creating swells on the surface. Waves spread out in every direction travelling as fast as five hundred miles an hour. On open ocean the swell may only be a few feet high, but as it pours into shallow water and narrow bays, as it did in Point au Gaul, water rapidly grows into a sheer face engulfing everything in its path.

For several minutes Robert stood on an embankment watching several waves crumble homes and destroy a score of stages and sheds; listening to the roaring sea, splintering wood and rumbling beach gravel. Then he ran for home only to find the narrow roadway awash. Water splashed knee high pulling and draining strength in his legs. As it receded, he held the picket fence, then jumped into a garden and reached home through the back meadows. He found his father walking around his house which, through some freak of nature, still stood intact. "I think, Father," he said, "it's safer with the rest of the people up on the hill. They have a fire lit in the woods to warm the frightened children. Where's mother?"

His mother was safe at a neighbour's house on higher land where she tended a woman in childbirth.

Within twenty minutes both men reached a makeshift shelter on the hill, by now filled with sobbing children and panic-stricken families. Robert stayed about an hour before he and several friends returned to the cove to inspect damage and to search for missing persons. Others, shocked and numbed, lead children to refuge in the little schoolhouse on the hill.

As Robert looked over the waterfront, he was amazed the shoreline was so clean, as if scoured bare by some demonic monster. Familiar buildings were gone. "All the fishing sheds had disappeared. A heap of wreckage offshore contained parts of sheds, sections of homes, overturned dories, poles and pilings of wharves and stages, the whole mess tangled with nets and fishing gear, fence railings, barrels – everything families needed to live and work. I counted 23 fishing premises entirely or partly destroyed."

Robert Hillier at Point au Gaul, a few years after the 1929 tidal wave or tsunami devastated the community.

Several people were missing and presumed drowned. Hillier set out to search. "By now, ten o'clock, I figured there was little danger of another wave. The sea had settled back to flat calm, and the night was cloudless but chilly."

With his friend, Gilbert Cake, he walked along the beach to the debris-filled Point, a mile or so distant. Then, a body. The first one found was a neighbour, Mary Ann Walsh, entangled in rubble near the shore.

> We carried the battered body to the Church Hall which, as more victims were found, became a temporary morgue. It was near midnight when Gilbert and I located another. First we spotted a dory pulled in on the strand on two rollers. As we neared it, we saw a young boy lying across the dory thwart with his hands in death grip on the engine house cover. He was only five and how he and the dory got there, was never satisfactorily explained.

Eight people from Point au Gaul were lost on that terrifying November night. Washed out of their home set adrift by the wave were Elizabeth Hillier and her four grandchildren – Elizabeth, Verna, Thomas, and Henry, the boy found in the dory. Elizabeth and Mary Ann Walsh were drowned. Thomas G. Hillier, visiting his home town from St. John's, had gone to secure his father's trap skiff but was apparently struck in the forehead with a wharf railing and killed.

Robert Hillier recalled the trauma of finding and preparing for burial those he had known so well: "You know, it was the hardest thing I ever did in my life. But in that time of death and destruction all bodies were found and given a proper Christian burial. A need to recover all the lost ones kept us together in the hours after. In the midst of death there is life for two babies were born the same night, one before the wave and one several hours after. This, too, helped us keep going that night."

From the peninsula's eastern side all communication to the rest of Newfoundland was cut off. Two days later the government coastal boat *Daisy* relayed news of the disaster to St. John's and within a week much needed assistance – food, supplies, medical attention, building materials – came from all corners of North America.

Slowly devastated communities like Point au Gaul rebuilt and, in time, their people recovered and then adjusted to other setbacks: the economic depression of the nineteen thirties, the provincial government's resettlement plan of the sixties. But the terrifying clash of nature's forces was never entirely forgotten by those, like Robert Hillier, who lived through it.

Point au Gaul today. In the foreground once stood the two room school where residents took refuge from the sea. At Point A, one of the tidal wave victims was entangled in debris; at B, Robert Hillier stood and watched a monster wave destroy a score of fishing sheds.

The Mysterious Springheel Jack and The Jumping Contest

A man once showed up in Fleur de Lys claiming he could out jump anyone around. It was a challenge not to be taken lightly. Someone would have to defeat this strange boaster. The event could have been a high jump, but in this case he challenged anyone in the town to a broad jump – distance over the ground either from a running or a standing start. The stranger is only known today by his nickname – Springheel (or Spring Hill) Jack.

The legends of Springheel Jack appear occasionally in Newfoundland tales. Author and songwriter Otto Kelland, who composed the well-known folk song "Let Me Fish off Cape St. Mary's," knew about him and wrote a story of Springheel's exploits in his book *Newfoundland Stories: Strange and Curious*. Springheel put in a surprise acrobatic appearance in St. John's and was seen jumping from rooftop to rooftop on Merrymeeting Road. No one seemed to know who this mysterious character was, where he came from or why he could leap so springingly. Those who read Stephen King's horror novels and short stories have also met a more sinister Springheel Jack in King's short story "Strawberry Spring."

Sporting events get lots of publicity today – the Olympics of summer and winter, World Cups, Stanley, Davis, Grey Cups, bonspiels, matches and scores of other international challenges. Games and contests are closely followed all over the world. But what of outport Newfoundland about one hundred years ago? Did our hardy pioneers have the time and the skill and would anyone in Fleur de Lys take up Springheel's challenge?

The well protected harbour of Fleur de Lys, the most northerly community on the Baie Verte Peninsula, was first established as a French fishing station near the prolific grounds called Petite Nord. In the harbour there's a striking rock formation over eight hundred feet high which has three hummocks or hills resembling a fleur de lis or lys, a three-leafed plant and the national symbol of France.

Fleur de Lys, as one of 40 French fishing stations along Newfoundland's French shore, rose in prominence. In 1706 the station had been the site of a clash between French and English interests. The *Falkland*, the *Nonsuch* and the *Medway*, all British warships, had been dispatched to the Petit Nord to protect British interests on petition of the "inhabitants of St. John's." Off Fleur de Lys harbour they

Aerial view of Fleur de Lys where a strange event took place many years ago.

exchanged fire with *Le Duc d'Orleans*, a ship of 30 guns and 110 men from St. Malo.

Between 1800 and 1850, a growing need to protect the interests of the French fishery year round was met in the hiring of gardiens for Fleur de Lys. The French presence at Fleur de Lys continued on mostly friendly terms, until the 1880s when English settlers predominated. Today some of the well-established family names in the town of 300 people are Walsh, Shea, Shelley, Traverse, Lewis and Barrett. The latter name may have been French in origin and spelled Ballett. Ancestors of the Barretts were fluent in French.

And what does all of this have to do with a jumping contest? On one old French map of Fleur de Lys there's a spot marked in French which roughly translates into English – The Jumping Place. According to local lore, this field or area (located today near Gordon Lewis' land on Harbour View Road) is where young people gathered to pass leisure time, specifically in feats of athletic ability. It was there Springheel Jack's jumping contest would take place.

The local gentleman who rose to the occasion was none other than Edward "Ned" Barrett of Fleur de Lys. Ned was one of the best. Perhaps that's why Springheel Jack showed up; maybe he heard just how good Ned Barrett was and wanted to take him on in a jump or two. It was known in the area that Ned, as a teenager and then as a young man, would rather leap over a fence than go through the gate. He was also known to line up a dozen fish barrels and with both feet together, hop in and out of each barrel in the line.

Another time while berry picking on Pigeon Island near Fleur de Lys, Ned's boat became untied and drifted to the mainland side of the tickle. Not wanting to get wet that day he leaped from a standing position, as there was no room to run, and landed on the cuddy of his boat on the other side – a distance of about eighteen feet.

On the day of the contest Ned Barrett, not knowing the ability of Springheel Jack, jumped first in a broad jump or as it is known in the Olympics today – the long jump. The mysterious challenger beat him. The second jump would be the final one and a conclusive statement of who was the best.

To everyone's surprise – and no doubt most of Fleur de Lys' folk were there to watch – Ned asked, "Mr. Springheel, how much do you weigh?"

When he learned Springheel was ten pound heavier, Ned said, "I'll carry two rocks, one in each pocket, to make our weigh even. But this time you go first."

Springheel's broad jump from a running or standing start was good, but on that day Ned Barrett cleared the former's mark by a wide margin, won the challenge and celebrated with the good people of Fleur de Lys.

The mysterious Springheel Jack slunk away with his tail between his legs; perhaps he took on no more human challenges after that and went to St. John's leaping roof to roof. Maybe he went back home, perhaps to Springhill, Nova Scotia, to jump never no more.

But the fate of Ned Barrett, sadly, has been documented by his kin in Fleur de Lys. According the story passed on by the late John T. Barrett to his son Kevin, Ned was lost at sea in the area of the Flemish Cap while he was a sailor on the foreign-going tern schooner *Evelyn*. He rose before eight, washed, shaved and prepared to take his turn at the wheel. There were no wheelhouses in those days, so Ned lashed himself to the wheel as was the custom during storms on the high seas.

A short time later a rogue wave swept the deck. Another man working up in the rigging clung on, but the force of hundreds of pounds of water ripped the wheel from its iron fastenings on the deck and carried it and Ned overboard. As reported by the captain and crew who rushed on deck when the alarm sounded, Ned Barrett freed himself from the ropes and the heavy wheel which was dragging him under.

Being a superb athlete, the young man was a strong swimmer and he was visible for a long time from the

This is the ship Ned Barrett sailed on when he was lost at sea. The 167-ton *Evelyn*, a tern or three-masted schooner, was ownedby Crosbie and Company, a fish exporting business based in St. John's. Three flags fly from the mastheads: on the foremast, Crosbie's red C on a white background; mainmast, the ship's name; and on the mizzenmast, the British flag.

Evelyn. His shipmates did everything possible to save Ned – throwing ropes with barrels attached hoping he could reach and cling on, but it was not to be. The schooner was running out of control with no steerage and it would be impossible to launch a lifeboat in the high winds and seas.

The captain of the *Evelyn* spoke highly of Ned Barrett, saying Newfoundland could not produce a more able seaman and that his death at sea was a great loss. He was drowned on February 20, 1911, two years before the year schooner *Evelyn* was wrecked at Ferryland. The memory of Ned lives on, especially of the day he defeated Springheel Jack at the Jumping Place in Fleur de Lys.

Up in Flames

After a few minutes inside the hall she and I started to dance when all of a sudden there was a great shouting near the stage and then fire was all over the ceiling near the stage. My dancing partner left saying her girlfriend was up there. I don't believe she got out.

For Herb Miller, what began as a night of relaxation turned quickly to one of tragedy and trauma. On December 12, 1942, he was a young Canadian serviceman on shore leave in St. John's. He survived a deadly fire and later wrote his recollections which he calls *The Fire at the St. John's Knights of Columbus*. Miller remembered that "Although many people lost their lives in that fire, my friends and I were among the lucky ones. Most of the dead were service people."

Today it might be called terrorism. But back then no one called the fire at the Knights of Columbus Hostel accidental. In the days and months following December 12, 1942, when an inferno levelled the K of C Hostel or servicemen's recreation centre on Harvey Road, official comments on its cause ranged from "suspicious" and "a result of arson" to the more damning "sabotage" and "subversive activity." Ninety-nine died, one hundred seven were injured, and a one hundred thousand dollar building was gobbled up in flames.

Until the 1980s it was, according to *The Monitor*, a Roman Catholic publication, the most tragic indoor fire ever in Newfoundland or Canada. The Knights of Columbus Hostel, a two-storey wooden building, was on that cold December evening, the location of the radio broadcast of "Uncle Tim's Barn Dance," a popular Saturday night rendevous for local girls, Royal Navy sailors, RCAF, American soldiers, other servicemen, and civilians young and old.

More than 450 people packed the building that night. Local entertainer Biddy O'Toole had just finished "I Met Her in the Garden Where the Praddies Grow" and a Canadian soldier, Eddie Adams, was yodelling "Moonlight Trail" when the building burst into flames. Inward-opening exit doors and plywood blackout shutters on windows, mandatory in a prominent seaport steeped in war-time activity, made escape difficult.

Miller, a diver and photographer on the RCN escort ship *Melville* which had put into St. John's in the morning to refuel, had shore leave until 1:00 A.M. that Saturday night. He met a friend Bill Noble, who was from Miller's home town of Durham, Ontario, and with several other sailors "took off for uptown to a concert and dance at the K of C Hall. It was broadcast on VOCM radio as the Barn Dance. This program was very popular and was listened to by ships at sea as well as the whole island of Newfoundland. Biddy O'Toole's band played real Newfoundland music."

They walked up Longs Hill in complete darkness. Miller says that lights in windows and doors were not allowed and windows had to be completely covered with blackout curtains. There were no streetlights. Car headlights had to be hooded and taped over with black tape with only a narrow slit to show light.

"The reason for the blackouts," Miller says, "was that well-lit cities could be seen for miles at sea and enemy subs were using the glow to outline ships and make them easier targets for night time torpedo attacks."

Cars were scarce in St. John's at this time and with no taxi available, the group had to walk up a slippery, snow-covered hill. A few too many slugs of ships' grog further jeopardized walking conditions.

By the time Miller and his group reached the K of C Hall, two of the group were worse for wear and their buddies found beds for them in the hostel part of the hall. Bed, mattress and blankets cost twenty-five cents for a serviceman.

Herb Miller finally got into the hall, found a girl and had danced when, sometime between ten-thirty and ten forty-five, shouts of a fire set panic in the crowd. He continued his story:

> Then the lights went out and the shouting really got loud. I was still near the door where I had come in when a big soldier turned on his flashlight and ripped the blackout curtains from the doorway and opened the door.
>
> Scores of people got out that door and the soldier saved many lives. Other doors out of the hall were bolted and as far as I know only one door was open.
>
> It happened so fast that when I got out on the street, the blackout curtains were burning off the windows and people inside could be seen trying to get out. I began to wonder if Bill Noble and our other crew members made it especially the two we put to bed in the hostel. This part (of the U-shaped building) was by now on fire as well.

Miller said it was impossible to find anyone in the milling crowds and he decided to go back down to the ship to see if any shipmates had shown up. They hadn't. *Melville's* captain sent him back to the scene to search for two of the missing men who were the top operators on the vessel's submarine detection apparatus. The ship, slated to depart at two A.M., couldn't sail without them.

> By this time the tons of water being poured on the fire was running down the hill and freezing which made my progress very slow.
>
> Hundreds of people were crowded near the fire, some crying, others shouting out names. Now the whole building was a mass of fire. A big heap of bodies was near the doorway I had escaped from – a sight one does not soon forget.

It was impossible for Miller to find out if any of his crew were in the crowd or if they were among the victims. After half an hour he went back aboard *Melville* and to his relief found all hands aboard. Miller was still worried about friend Bill Noble. Before he sailed he called his house, but Bill had not turned up there. But, there was little time for a ship on convoy duty has strict sailing orders and *Melville* pulled out of the harbour.

"That night," wrote Miller, "for many miles from Newfoundland, the glow in the sky from the fire was visible and I worried about Bill."

Herb's ship sailed to the south shore of Greenland and joined the escort group to convoy some thirty-five ships bound for the United States. In New York he says, "I got a big bunch of mail from home, letters from Mother and a bundle of *Durham Chronicle* newspapers. The papers said a Durham boy, Cecil Brown, was badly injured in the fire and still hospitalized. There was no word about Bill Noble."

On duty between Britain, Greenland and North America, several weeks passed before the *Melville* re-visited St. John's; thus the official inquiry in the Hostel fire, led by Supreme Court Justice Sir Brian Dunfield, did not call Miller to testify.

Dunfield had examined 174 witnesses in the St. John's Courthouse, and guardedly concluded the Knights of Columbus fire was of "suspicious... incendiary origin" probably caused by an inflammatory agitator who sets fire to an enemy's buildings.

Miller, with a group of other Ontario boys, went to visit Cecil Brown, recuperating from severe burns to the back of his head and shoulders. He learned that Bill Noble had gotten out of the burning building unharmed and mingled in the crowd – estimated by some to be ten thousand – watching the fire.

Today Herb Miller, a veteran of World War II and a survivor of one of the deadliest fires in Canadian history, lives in Durham where he wrote his previously unpublished memoirs of the K of C Hostel disaster.

The K of C fire, December 12, 1942.

PUBLISHING HISTORY

For their support and encouragement of my writing efforts, I wish to thank the editors of each publication in which my stories appeared. To readers who called or wrote with comments, questions, requests concerning my writings in those publications, I also express my appreciation. I would like to dedicate this volume to those editors/publishers who evaluated what I was trying to say, gave perceptive advice, and eventually put my writings "in print." Several come to mind: Don Morgan, George Mcvicar, Harry Cuff and sons, Janice Stuckless, Paula Gale, Jillian Power and Bruce Ricketts.

1. "Bound Home for Newfoundland": Unpublished.
2. "Every Man for Himself": Unpublished
3. "The *Titanic*, the *Majestic* and the *Antelope*": Published in *The Southern Gazette* April 13, 1999.
4. "Saved by a Horse": First published as "*Nordica* – Newfoundland's Mary Celeste" in *The Newfoundland Quarterly*, Winter 1989.
5. Heroes at Lumsden Beach": Unpublished.
6. "Race to St. Pierre": First published in *Newfoundland Lifestyle* as "Cook Baker and the General" Vol.8, No.4 October 1990.
7. "Three Short Sentences": Published in *The Newfoundland Quarterly* Fall 1991 and in *Vignettes of a Small Town*, 1997.
8. "A Battle of the Atlantic": Published in the column "Times, Tides and Tales" on the internet site www.shipwrecks.nf.ca
9. "This War No Good, Jack": First published in *Legion Magazine* as "A Long Ways Out" July/August 1991.
10. "In the Line of Duty on HMS *Laurentic*": Published in *The Evening Telegram* June 29, 2003 and in The *Southern Gazette* June 30, 2003.
11. "The Unsolved Mystery of George's Island": Published on internet site "Mysteries of Canada" May 2003 and in January 2004 *Downhomer*.
12. "Oh Brother, Passion and Anger: Murder in Small Town Newfoundland": Unpublished

13. "I'm Glad I Did It: Murder in Shore's Cove, Cape Broyle": Unpublished.

14. "Running the Blockade": Published in the column "Born Down by the Ocean" in the internet newspaper *Watermarks* April 2002 (now defunct).

15. "Send Extra Police – Immediately": Published in *The Southern Gazette*, December 27, 1994, and submitted to the Arts and Letters Awards, St. John's.

16. "The Warship *Cornwall* and the Siege of Flat Island": Unpublished.

17. "Wall of Water": Published in *Newfoundland Lifestyle* Spring 1993.

18. "The Mysterious Springheel Jack": Published in *Downhomer* April 2002.

19. "Up in Flames": Published in *The Evening Telegram*, December 9, 2001.

NOTES

BOUND HOME FOR NEWFOUNDLAND

Last year I located a very brief clipping in a local paper of Philip Osmond's voyage to Newfoundland. I was astounded at Philip's long, dangerous odyssey in a small boat, but could find very little material in archives or local papers on his feat.

I put out a request for information in the print media and several people wrote, e-mailed or called with information about the family, their ship and the journey to Newfoundland. I am grateful to these correspondents for providing stories, notes and/or photos: Mrs. Mildred Osmond, wife of the late Sterling Osmond, Lethbridge; Scott Harris, Lethbridge; Shirley (Osmond) Martin; St. Phillips; Lewis Collins, Hare Bay; Fred Hancock, St. John's; Gladys Kelloway, Victoria; NL; Evelyn (Osmond) Killam, Moncton, NB; Floyd Osmond, NB; Stella Brown, Peterborough, ON; Fraser Rideout and Mildred Rideout, Toronto, ON; and Carson Stratton, Pickering, ON.

Of course I have to acknowledge the dedication of the staff at the Newfoundland Reference Room at the A. C. Hunter Library, St. John's, for this story and many others I have researched. In no time they had ordered in and made available the PEI papers and the *Toronto Star* for May 1938.

EVERY MAN FOR HIMSELF

In the 1970s Captain John Marshall Fudge of Belleoram published his interesting and unique autobiography in 60-page book, John Marshall Fudge: *His Life as a Fishermen and Businessman*, Atlas Press, Moncton. His memoirs had a limited publication run and has long since gone out of print. Marshall, as he writes in his book, had many close calls on the sea. He was run down in a dory by his own schooner, endured stormy voyages, saw his crewmen washed overboard, and survived the inevitable shipwreck. After abandoning the sea and living the United States for several years, in the 1930s he came back home to Belleoram and purchased the 29-ton schooner *Geneva Ethel* from Jeremiah Petite of English Harbour West.

According to a *Daily News* report of September 11, 1935, *Geneva Ethel* arrived at Pushthrough to report seaman Abraham Tibbo had been washed overboard in the heavy seas and drowned.

This tale of the sea comes from two sources: the newspaper account of the August Gale of 1935 and Captain Fudge's story in which he identifies the lost seaman as Philip Tibbo.

THE *TITANIC*, THE *MAJESTIC* AND THE *ANTELOPE*

Several years ago I had many discussions and informal chats about local history with Curtis Forsey, who at that time was in his nineties and a resident of the Agnes Pratt Home. Born and raised in Grand Bank, for a brief period in the 1930s he ran a branch of his father's salt fish exporting business at Epworth, near Burin.

He had often heard the local tales of shipwreck and disaster of Burin and Epworth. One in particular tale he recalled was the one told of White Star ocean liner *Majestic* that cut down the Burin schooner *Antelope* in 1894. Forsey had heard that Captain Edward Smith (later captain of the *Titanic*) was in command of *Majestic* at the time. Intrigued I went to the library and researched the life of Smith to determine if he were *Majestic*'s captain when it rammed the *Antelope.*

That search lead me to think of other Newfoundland connections with the White Star Line, the *Titanic*, and other collisions at sea. Eventually this piece was published in the Burin Peninsula newspaper *Southern Gazette.*

As well as the personal conversation with Curtis Forsey, Grand Bank, who knew of the incident of William Woundy and the boxer James J. Corbett, I also talked with John Peacock of Navan, Ontairo, a descendant of the Bugdens of Burin. Newfoundland newspapers of the day carried short versions of the story. *New York Times* of August 2, 1894, and *The Halifax Herald* August 6, 1894, had lengthy accounts of the collision. To determine what ships Smith commanded I found that Gary Cooper's *The Man Who Sank Titanic* (Wittan Books, 1992) to be the most informative source.

SAVED BY A HORSE

It has been said that practically everything and anything that could happen has happened to a Newfoundland schooner: piracy, fire, mutiny, disappearances, unexplained explosions, rammings, rum running, pursuit and capture by the American coast guard and collisions with icebergs. Some schooners were struck by lightning, shelled by enemy submarines, crushed by Arctic ice, swallowed up by "August Gales" or other violent windstorms, and many were stranded and wrecked. Fishermen in their banking dories rowed away from the mother ship to disappear forever in the cold Atlantic fog. Schooners sank in the vast expanse of the North Atlantic, their rescued crews taken by foreign ships to strange and remote ports, and left to get back home the best way they could. These were the lucky ones. Dozens of schooners with their crews disappeared without a trace. This is a story of another odd or unique happening on a Newfoundland vessel – a ship abandoned with no just cause or logical reason.

"Saved by a Horse" was my first story of the sea published in a magazine: *The Newfoundland Quarterly*, Winter 1989. For the purpose of *Born Down by the Water* I re-typed the story (which was originally called "*Nordica* – Newfoundland's *Mary Celeste*), added introductory material, crew lists, and other relevant information. Author's Afterword: The first inkling I had of this amazing tale came from Curtis Forsey, who knew *Nordica*'s second captain, "Pluck" Tibbo, and from him Forsey had learned verbally the story of abandonment and salvage. When I read the articles on the initial loss of *Nordica* in *The Evening Telegram* (November 9 and 27, 1920) which gave an approximate date of its arrival in Boston, I sent a letter to the Boston newspaper archives, hoping to get newspaper articles of the abandonment from that end. I received *Boston Globe* and *Boston Herald* for November 3, 1920, and that give details of the discovery of an abandoned ship by SS *Western Comet*. Newspaper *Fishermen's Advocate* (December 7, 1932) had a summary called "Shipping Casualties of Newfoundland and Nova Scotian Vessels from January 1920 to March 1921" and this pinpointed, with the article of *Daily News* November 26, 1921, the exact place and circumstances of *Nordica*'s second death.

Helpful in the research was George Barnes' daughter, Mary (Barnes) Hillier. One of the final pieces of the puzzle came from Gilbert Tibbo of Gander who knew the story and supplied the crew list of *Nordica* when it was lost on Corsica.

HEROES AT LUMSDEN BEACH

Dear Mr. Abbott, Stewart:

I have to write to say how much I enjoyed the evening we spent together, chatting in your home in Gander. Our talk of sail, ships and seamen was truly invigorating, especially from one, like yourself, who has had so many experiences on the sea and in life.

As you will no doubt recall, the story of the wreck of *Alice M. Pike* came as a result of your phone call to me in the spring of 2001 when you said you had two or three shipwrecks stories I might be interested in. I certainly was interested and what stories they turned out to be. And best of all each had happened to you personally.

Since that time I have completed the story of the loss of "*Alice M. Pike*" although in the future there may be some other gaps we may yet fill. There is quite a difference in the bare two-sentence description in the newspaper of the day and the vivid description you provided. Yours is more powerful, detailed and filled with nuggets of important information – details that will, in the future, help Newfoundlanders and Labradorians understand our history a little more.

Of course, as my writing of the story progressed I had to check back with you with several times to ask for particulars, names of crew and rescuers, and specifics about the wrecked ship. You were so helpful and patient. If, when reading over this story, you have any questions call me.

Finally, I hope you enjoy the story. I know your account of the exciting events on "*Alice M. Pike*" over fifty years ago will eventually be published for all to read.

Someday soon my wife and I will be back to visit you and Gladys. Tell her I appreciated the hospitality, the cups of tea and sea yarns of one – a man of the deep – who has salt water flowing in his veins.

Regards and I'll be seeing you soon,

Robert

RACE TO ST. PIERRE

"Race to St. Pierre" was written in the summer of 1990 for two very different and diametrically opposed reasons: love and money. Well, maybe they're related. Anyway, my Uncle Bill Baker happily recounted with considerable flair, his sea stories – those he had been involved in directly. It was my pleasure to listen and, later, to record them. Up until he was in his eighties, he had clear memories of numerous incidents on the sea, dozens of which happened to him and, in addition, he could recall stories others had told him of their marine experiences. When I asked him about his voyages on the tern schooner *General Wood*, at first he summarized his misadventure in one sentence as "I was washed off the deck of that one once, but I survived." When I asked him to be more specific, the actual memoir resulted in a richly detailed and unique story. It was because of admiration for the hardy seamen like Uncle Bill, I wrote his story and sent it to a magazine for publication.

This sea yarn was originally entitled "Cook Baker and the General." It became my second article published by *Newfoundland Lifestyle* and I received ten cents a word, almost double what I was paid for my first article (which incentive enough to write the second one, wasn't it?).

Due to length requirement or space restrictions which govern such magazines, I had to cut two introductory paragraphs and delete other relevant information within the story. In *Born Down by the Water* there's the complete version.

THREE SHORT SENTENCES

As a high school student in the early 1960s, I tried to get down to studying geometry theorems and geography in the kitchen, a place often frequented by my father's friends who came to visit him "after supper." One man in particular told fascinating sea stories; in fact often he repeated many particularly gruelling and spellbinding yarns. It was hard for me to keep attention focussed on school books.

In June 1987, when I began to search out Grand Bank's numerous sea stories and oral re-tellings of tragedy and heroism, I went to see the same veteran seaman who had been to my father's home nearly thirty years previously. I asked if he would retell some of the yarns; sadly his mind was not as keen, but he recalled, sketchily, stories of his true experiences.

In February 1990 I sent his version (with the section on the chocolate box and notebook embellished) of the sinking of the *Jean McKay* to the magazine *The Newfoundland Quarterly*. It was second of my sea stories submitted to be published in that magazine. But I heard nothing from the editor for months. Then out of the blue, almost two years later, a large brown envelope came in the mail; inside, a copy of 1991 fall edition of *The Quarterly* and there was the story. *The Newfoundland Quarterly* pays contributors a small honorarium, but the satisfaction of seeing George's story in print far outweighed any monetary gain.

A BATTLE OF THE ATLANTIC

In January 2001 I set up a website on the internet at the URL http://shipwrecks.nf.ca. Websites are of little value unless someone goes to the site and reads or reacts to the information posted there. There's a new maxim for this: Your unchanging static website is like an albatross hanging around your neck. It does more harm than good for once a reader visits, there has to be something to bring the visitor back.

To remedy this I publish a historical/marine column "Times, Tides and Tales" which changes every two months i.e. bi-monthly. The following story, posted on the internet in July 2003, was my sixteenth sea story on the site.

THIS WAR NO GOOD, JACK

Several years ago I sent an inquiry, an idea, for a sea story to a national magazine. To my way of thinking the clash of an enemy sub with a small defenceless schooner would be a topic of national interest. I mailed the story, unsolicited, to *Legion Magazine*, a magazine published in Ontario. Its audience is mainly war veterans and the military. *Legion Magazine* has one of the highest magazine circulations in Canada, trailing publications like *McLeans* and *Reader's Digest*. The editor was quick to point out *Legion* did not often publish stories of actual war events – battles, skirmishes, deaths and so on. But since the story elaborated on how the German sailors looked and acted as viewed by Newfoundland seamen, it was accepted and published as "A Long Ways Out."

IN THE LINE OF DUTY

I am a firm believer that books, like tickets for a dance, don't sell themselves. If no one knows an event is happened who will attend? The same can be said for books – get out and meet the book-buying public. I do. At every opportunity.

A year or so ago while standing behind a booth in Clarenville promoting – or 'flogging' as some might say – books, a young man stopped to ask if I knew of the sinking of the *Laurentic*. I didn't. He went on to tell me that his grandfather's brother perished when the great ship struck a mine during WWI and how the ship was carrying gold. And, he said, there was high loss of life including several other Newfoundlanders. The idea, feeling, urge, that there was a sea tale to be told took a grip on my psyche and wouldn't let go until I had written this one.

Help in the research of this tale of the sea came from William Hooper of Chance Cove. Samuel Hooper was his grandfather's brother. Gerry Keegan of British Columbia lost a grandfather on *Laurentic* and his work, as well as information from Newfoundland archival newspapers and the British Admiralty Court inquiry, enabled me finish the account.

THE UNSOLVED MYSTERY OF GEORGE'S ISLAND

In October 2003 the editor of Newfoundland's folksy but highly regarded and well-appreciated magazine *Downhomer* called to ask me for a marine-related story for its issue on Labrador. That issue was due to be published in January 2004, giving me a lead time of three months. Stories are often submitted to magazines and newspapers two or three months ahead of actual publication date.

I suggested one or two possibilities, but the good editor, Janice Stuckless, became interested in a murder mystery that also involved a shipwreck which happened on a remote island off Labrador.

The story had also appeared on an internet site "Mysteries of Canada" which publishes stories from all regions of our country. Knowing the audience likely to read the story at that site would be limited, I felt its inclusion here in *Born Down By The Water* (and in *Downhomer*) would be give it more exposure and perhaps a greater chance to the solution of the mystery.

Since this story was first published, Hudson Bay records reveal that *Walrus's* survivor was Andrew Corneaux.

OH BROTHER, PASSION AND ANGER

While gathering material for this collection of stories, I consulted many individuals for information and read through much archival material. I found this next story intriguing, not only for the details of the crime and the ensuing trial, but it gives us a chance to look back at Newfoundland to another time and other circumstances. Economic conditions, the state of the fishery, homes and landmarks have changed, but human characteristics have not.

For those who are interested in such things, I began this story in January 2003 and completed the first draft in February. After much second thought and debate about who could be hurt or affected by this tale of wrong doing, I decided to include it, as much for the history and the glimpse into the life of fishermen of a century ago, as for the tragic details of murder and mayhem. It became one of the last stories written for this volume.

RUNNING THE BLOCKADE

The story of our defiant pioneers in the Fortune Bay skirmish came from several sources. I first became aware of the uprising when I talked to Curtis Forsey. I also spoke with George Foote, Grand Bank, who knew about the effects of the Bait Act and related the tale of the *Smuggler*. References to the Bait Act can be found in Newfoundland history books including J.A. Cochrane's *The Story of Newfoundland*. Local historian Aaron Buffett mentions the problems with enforcing the Bait Act in his history of Grand Bank. These pioneers are gone from us now, but they were the ones who vigorously opposed unjust laws.

As I wished to find a more human element i.e. the names of those who had the determination to oppose unfair legislation and to clash with authority, I searched the papers of the day to find exactly who had been arrested. There were articles in *The Evening Telegram* August 3, 1888, April 20 and 22, May 2 and 10, 1891, and *Evening Herald* April 29 and May 2, 1891. While looking through back issues of *Atlantic Guardian* (January 1949), I saw a paragraph which quoted a policeman who actually went to Fortune Bay to quell the insurrection. This tale, then, is taken from a combination of oral and written accounts.

SEND EXTRA POLICE – IMMEDIATELY

I had been submitting stories, prose and poetry to the Newfoundland Arts and Letters Competition since 1989. In 1995, this entry placed second in the Non-Fiction Prose category. The contest judge suggested that "since the subject is both fascinating and important, I recommend the author submit it for publication."

This is a tale of how not to do things, or if events and radical changes are not well-planned some unnecessary reactions will follow, sort of like Newton's Third Law – For every action there is an equal and opposite reaction. The actions in this tale however deal with people and their lives.

THE WARSHIP *CORNWALL*
AND THE SIEGE OF FLAT ISLAND

Readers, you will, no doubt, see that this is the third story in this collection of a rebellion or a resistance to authority by our Newfoundland people. Perhaps in shame or through embarrassment, this aspect – resistance or civil disobedience which begat lawlessness – of our island history is not much written nor talked about.

To me, the stands against authority represent a fierce independence nurtured by a hardy life on a remorseless land – a land fought for with sweat and lives. These tales of a different type of heroism are just as important as the struggles to wrest a livelihood from the ocean.

This story was derived from newspapers of the day: *Evening Advocate* July 5 and 24, 1919; *The Evening Telegram*'s "The Cruise of the HMS *Cornwall*" July 7, 1919, and an unidentified newspaper clipping of July 8, 1919, with the heading, "The Flat Island Trial." The archives at Memorial University (Collection 285.2.06.011, pages 150-152) confirmed the identity of the young pistol-packing reporter who went to Flat Island on board the warship.

WALL OF WATER

Each year around November 18, stories and personal accounts of the tidal wave which devastated southern portions of Newfoundland makes the news on radio, local television or in the newspapers. It is one of the most talked about and interest-generating events in local history.

My late father-in-law, Robert Hillier, was an impressionable nineteen year old on that memorable November night. Like many others who lived through it, he never forgot the details of the great wave that pounded his village of Point au Gaul. Point au Gaul not only had the greatest number of deaths attributed to the wave, but it was one of the smallest towns. As well, the entire waterfront of fishing stages and wharves was wiped out.

One day he and I talked at some length about the tidal wave. He could recall so much of this ordeal that I thought it imperative to "write it down." In 1993 I sent the story, with Robert's (or the Skipper, as he was affectionately called) permission, to *Newfoundland Lifestyle*, but somehow the wrong date of the tidal wave was printed in the magazine. Needless to say, I received unwanted fan mail. The version here has the correct date and other added details learned after the story was published.

THE MYSTERIOUS SPRINGHEEL JACK
AND THE JUMPING CONTEST

For the background to this story I am grateful to Kevin Barrett of Fleur de Lys who wrote me to tell the details of his great-uncle Ned

Barrett's drowning from a ship in mid-Atlantic. However his great-uncle Ned, as Kevin knew, was also a good athlete in Fleur de Lys. I was much intrigued by Ned's encounter with a strange and mysterious opponent in an athletic contest.

In February 2002 I sent the tale to the *Downhomer* magazine where it appeared in April's issue as "The Jumping Contest." The title is much longer here for I wished to include the name of the elusive Springheel Jack. For those of you who write stories or articles for magazines it's great to have an interesting topic, but when you can combine two ideas – as in this one, the mysterious character, and the life and death of Ned Barrett – into one story, it's all the better.

UP IN FLAMES

Herb Miller of Durham, Ontario, was dancing in the Knights of Columbus Hall on December 12, 1942, when a fire broke out that killed 99 people. He escaped and helped rescue others; yet he was not called to testify at the Dunfield inquiry into the cause of the tragic fire. Herb's ship, directly involved with convoy protection, left port that same night and he didn't return until several months after the inquiry was over.

Herb sent me his story and later we talked in some length over the telephone. His recollection was a tale not only of the fire, but of his views of St. John's at a time when the threat of war and espionage put a new perspective on life in the city. This story appeared in *The Evening Telegram* on December 9, 2001.

ACKNOWLEDGEMENTS

Stewart Abbott of Gander/Musgrave Harbour
The late William Baker of Grand Bank
Kevin Barrett of Fleur de Lys
Norman Crane of St. John's
The late George Foote of Grand Bank
The late Curtis Forsey of Grand Bank
The late John Marshall Fudge in "His Life as a Fisherman" of Belleoram
Fred Hancock of St. John's/Lethbridge
The late L. Robert Hillier of Grand Bank/Point au Gaul
William Hooper of Chance Cove
Herb Miller of Durham, ON
The Osmond family
The late Teddy Pardyof Grand Bank
John Peacock of Navan, ON
Clayton Rogers of Grand Bank

PHOTO PAGES	CREDIT
3, 23, 38, 60 (top left), 122	Robert Parsons
5	Mildred Osmond
16	Flanker Press
18	John Peacock
32, 33	James Seaward
43	George Squires
51	Robert Stoodley
60 (top right)	William Hooper
60 (bottom)	Hubert Hall, Shipsearch (MARINE)
65, 124	Deptartment of Natural Resources, Surveys, and Mapping
88	A.C. Hunter Library, Photographic Coll.
90, 127	Maritime History Archives, MUN
102	Margaret Tibbo
106	Neil Locke
107	Helen and Hazel Milley
113	Internet site
115	Jack Feltham
120	The Hillier Family
132	PANL, St. John's

INDEX

148